Reimagining the Classroom

Reimagining the Classroom

Creating New Learning Spaces and Connecting with the World

Theodore Richards

Published by Jossey-Bass

A Wiley Imprint

John Wiley & Sons, Inc., 111 River Street, Hoboken, NJ 07030, USA

Jossey-Bass books and products are available through most bookstores. To contact Jossey-Bass directly call our Customer Care Department within the U.S. at 800-956-7739, outside the U.S. at 317-572-3986, or fax 317-572-4002.

Jossey-Bass also publishes its books in a variety of electronic formats. Some content that appears in print may not be available in electronic books.

Library of Congress Cataloging-in-Publication Data:

Names: Richards, Theodore, author.
Title: Reimagining the classroom : creating new learning spaces and connecting with the world / Theodore Richards.
Description: First edition. | Hoboken, NJ : Jossey-Bass, 2023. | Includes bibliographical references and index.
Identifiers: LCCN 2022031901 (print) | LCCN 2022031902 (ebook) | ISBN 9781119877042 (paperback) | ISBN 9781119877059 (adobe pdf) | ISBN 9781119877066 (epub)
Subjects: LCSH: Educational change—United States. | Education—Aims and objectives—United States.
Classification: LCC LA217.2 .R53 2023 (print) | LCC LA217.2 (ebook) | DDC 370—dc23/eng/20220812
LC record available at https://lccn.loc.gov/2022031901
LC ebook record available at https://lccn.loc.gov/2022031902

COVER DESIGN: PAUL MCCARTHY
COVER ART: © ISTOCKPHOTO | PROKSIMA

SKY10037480_102622

This book is dedicated to the youth of the Chicago Wisdom Project.

"I cannot be a teacher without exposing who I am."

—Paulo Freire

Contents

Introduction: Everything Is Education; Everywhere Is a Classroom

A child sits alone, staring at a screen.

This is the enduring image of the COVID pandemic: the sad and lonely child, learning "remotely." It is the child who encapsulates this moment, the child who forces a reckoning with the world we've made, the future we've mortgaged, the cost of our hubris. It is perhaps then the only logical consequence of this system that our children should end up this way: alone, staring at a screen. This loneliness a manifestation of a deeper, cosmic loneliness, the spirit of rugged independence made flesh.

Its cost is apparent to any parent. Every gift of childhood—joy, exploration, play, wonder—sacrificed at the altar of the system. And so, it is also odd that our response to this crisis is a doubling down, a deeper investment in the very system that birthed it.

But there is a gift in this crisis, even if some refuse to see it. The pandemic has shown us so many things that we've been doing are perhaps worth rethinking. Why do we prepare our children for work that will surely no longer exist, for a world that will be so radically changed? It has brought our children's schools into our homes, and we have been able to see just how impoverished their educational lives often are.

Obviously, remote learning isn't ideal. But we also can see that our school systems—like many systems—were already problematic long before that pandemic hit. Our children's lives were dominated by a narrow breadth of easily tested skills and information. Our children were already spending their days on screens, already in the midst of a mental health crisis.

This book is an invitation to look to our children as a way to find hope in a time of despair. It offers a vision of how we might reimagine teaching, learning, and parenting to a create a space for our children to reimagine our world. For the greatest mistake we could make right now (and this is indeed the mistake we are making with so many remote learning models) is to try to replicate the old way of doing things.

Let's return to our child, the remote learner. One of my children (at the time she was a seventh grader; the other two younger children were homeschooled for kindergarten and first grade) has been in such a program, so I can attest that the issue is neither the competence nor the effort of her teachers. The problem is that we've forgotten the key to education, to parenting and childhood—to humanity. We've forgotten that all learning, all growth, all life is *relational.*

You won't find buzzwords or educational jargon in this book. Rather, you'll find a lot of questions: you'll be asked to reimagine your relationship to others, to the world as a whole. The crisis is making it apparent that some of the basic assumptions we've made about the world are worth rethinking. Foremost among them is our sense of independence and isolation—from each other, from the world as a whole. Our schools are rooted in the values of independence and isolation, and the consequence is that we are increasingly lonely. The crises we face, from the pandemic to climate change to the struggle for racial justice, all call upon us to think holistically and *inter*dependently. You'll find here a framework for reimagining the basic narratives and metaphors upon which our schools—and, indeed, our civilization—are based, and practices that are rooted not only in my work homeschooling my own children, but also on decades of experience as an educator through the organization I founded.

My hope is that professional educators will use this book to reconsider how they are doing things in schools and that homeschooling parents will use it to create vibrant learning spaces at home. But I also hope that any parent or role model can use it to rethink the relationships they are cultivating in their homes and elsewhere. For among the many assumptions that the reader will be asked to re-evaluate in this book are the very notions of "classroom," "school," and "education."

A classroom or a school isn't merely a neutral space in which to perform the act of educating. The ways it is shaped, structured, and organized are rich with meaning, and most of that meaning is unarticulated, often unconscious. If the purpose of education is to create a better world, it is this unconscious symbolism of the school and classroom that provides us with a vision for the world our youth might create. In other words, the classroom is a microcosm, a metaphor for the world.

We will not only challenge this understanding of the classroom and the school, but also seek to think more expansively of what constitutes those spaces. The world can be a classroom; and everything can be understood as education. It is commonly said, for example, that when a society invests in prisons or the military and divests in schools, it is taking money from education in favor of those other institutions. And indeed, such decisions are a reflection of a society's values. But another way to frame such a decision is to say that whatever we invest in is, as a reflection of values, an investment in some form of education. To invest in a prison—and to incarcerate greater numbers of people—is to choose that space as a classroom, a space in which many will learn their place in the world. To invest in the military is to choose the values and worldview of the soldier.

Part I offers the reader a framework to develop vibrant and holistic learning spaces and processes. In Chapter 1, we will explore the problems with our current approach to teaching, parenting, and childhood. Specifically, the core metaphors and narratives upon which this system is based will be addressed and critiqued. Chapter 2 offers an alternative set of core metaphors giving the reader a framework from which to cultivate new kinds of learning spaces. Chapter 3 will describe a holistic process of inquiry and exploration, a pedagogy for reimagining our narratives.

Part II offers examples of specific practices drawn from my experience teaching my own children and creating programming through Wisdom Projects, Inc. Each chapter is a reimagined subject: Chapter 4 takes an approach to science and math that emphasizes hands-on experiences in nature, awe, and wonder, all rooted in the universe story; Chapter 5 focuses on the arts, including literature; Chapter 6 describes practices in meditation, mindfulness, and rites of passage rooted in philosophical and cultural traditions from around the world; Chapter 7 offers hands-on learning projects; and Chapter 8 integrates social justice and social-emotional learning.

Finally, Part III briefly explores what happens when the concepts and practices of our reimagined classroom are applied to the world. In short, we must not forget why we are educating in the first place: not merely to make better students, but better citizens, better human beings, better communities. A better world.

We have lost our sense of place in the world. The stories we've been given have taught us that we are alone and, ultimately, lonely. We live in a time of unprecedented crises, an age that requires unprecedented changes, not merely in our systems, but in the very values, ideas, and narratives that give us our sense of who we are and our place in the cosmos.

But most of us are too deeply embedded in our worldview to even be able to grasp the urgency and immensity of the changes required. We often simply cannot imagine what doesn't fit in our story. But there *is* hope. For there are people among us who aren't as invested in the worldview that has led us into so much trouble: our children. Our work, as parents and educators, is to create the spaces and facilitate the processes that can allow *them* to teach *us*. Our children, unlike us, will not hesitate to claim their new place in the world, if we can only offer them the space to do it—and the humility to listen.

Part I

Reimagining Education

Our learning process is rooted in the stories we tell and reimagine. Our learning spaces serve as metaphors for the world our children will create. In this section, we'll offer a critique of the metaphors of the current system and a method for educators to create their own vibrant learning spaces and activities. This includes both the way we conceive of a classroom and the processes therein.

We begin with a critique of the broader culture that our educational system has brought us, the underlying story that has alienated us from our fellow beings, human and non-human, and from the planet itself. This is an educational problem, for it is how we educate our children that gives them the story in the first place. And it is only by reimagining education that they might discover a new story. This story is given by the metaphors that guide the formation of a classroom. It is reimagined only when we transform those metaphors and enter into a learning process that engages the whole person, the whole community, the whole world.

Chapter 1

The Crisis of Education

Childhood in the Age of Loneliness

From the melting polar caps to violence in our cities to the rise of fascist governments, ours is an age in which we seem to be able to agree on almost nothing—except that we are in crisis. It would be easy to think of the rising anxiety I'm feeling as disconnected from the rising sea levels, or to think of the migrant crisis as unrelated to the violence in our inner cities. But at the core, all of our crises actually share some of the same roots, and part of the individual healing process involves exploring those roots collectively.

This book is about this global crisis, but it isn't about the melting polar caps, or CO_2 levels, or temperature.

It isn't about increasing economic disparities, racism, or sexism. It's about a climate of loneliness that has taken over the planet—a planet of shrinking resources, imagination, hope. But how can we be hopeful when news of our demise comes on the television every night? How can we learn to share our resources when we are told that we can only find meaning by consuming more? Most significantly, how can we live as though the planet itself is a single, interconnected community when we have been told that our purpose is to find only individual success, only individual salvation?

I suggest that our spiritual malaise—the loneliness and loss of meaning—is connected to our ecological, political, and economic crises. It's all connected; and it's all about the deep story we tell about who we are and our place in the world. And this all comes down to how we educate our children.

Let me explain.

There's something in the air, as thick and unmistakable as the CO_2 particulates, even if it isn't as easily quantified. All around us, there is an anxiety about our future, about the future of our children. And like climate change, this anxiety is so massive, so all-encompassing and -consuming, that it feels impossible to escape, impossible to confront.

We also live in an age of anger, and in an age of fear. But of all the emotions that dominate our age, I believe that *loneliness* is the most pervasive. It is loneliness that tortures the internet troll or Wall Street executive who never seems to have enough; it is loneliness that leads us to addictions to shopping or food or anti-anxiety meds.

In some ways, this is my greatest fear and, perhaps, that which we all fear: being alone, really alone. I've often suggested that this is the ultimate salvation we are all seeking—true communion, connection—far more than any lonely, segregated paradise.

Why are we lonely? The reasons are complex and have to do with the habits and lifestyles of the modern world. We spend less time with family and community; we spend more time staring at screens. But our loneliness begins with a story, a story about who we are on the most fundamental level. This story tells us that our deepest identity is individual, and that we need to buy our way into a meaningful life.

It's unmistakable how lonely we all are. You can feel it in crowds, among the masses of people ignoring one another, staring at their own privatized virtual space in favor of the physical world. How is it that I can feel less lonely alone in my living room, listening to Coltrane, than I do on a crowded bus? This feeling reveals to us that loneliness isn't entirely about being alone, at least not the kind of loneliness I am talking about. I am referring to more than the sadness at missing one's kin. This is a *cosmic* loneliness. This loneliness is the product of a narrative that tells us that our ultimate identity is individual, that we are not, in fact, in this together.

And we aren't just lacking in community with other people; we have lost our ecological place in the family of beings. We've lost our intimacy with the Earth—its rivers, its mountains, its seas—and the other species that make it up, that make us who we are. This requires us to experience the Earth in intimacy, not just stare at screens and drive from one sterile, climate-controlled space to another. It requires us to feel the texture of our world again, to fall in love again.

The climate crisis teaches us that we are an interconnected planet—decisions made on one continent impact another. Less widely considered is this crisis of the *inner* climate. This inner climate is, like the outer, interconnected. Our emotional lives are ecological webs, not isolated individuals. So, if the inner life is made toxic by a toxic story, we become unbalanced. I don't need to use extreme examples like mass shooters or oil spills here. Just spend some time on social media or watch the plastic bags floating down your street. There is something even more profound than the realization of our interconnectedness: *our emotions are a part of the ecosystem and a part of the Earth itself.*

And so, we must let go of the notion that loneliness—whether it's expressed on social media or by the person sitting in the cubical next to you, addicted to their meds—is merely an individual, psychological problem, a mental health issue. Loneliness, by its very nature, cannot be cured individually. It is a shared problem. It is a cultural problem. A problem of story.

OUR STORY

Think back to your earliest memories of childhood. What is one of the first stories you remember? If your childhood was like mine, you may recall curling up somewhere with a parent or another elder, listening to a story. Or perhaps you can recall attending a church or another place of worship and hearing the stories passed down through the generations. It was in these moments that you would have learned life's deepest and most important lessons. Through human touch, voice, and the magic of words, you began to put your world together. You began to discover your place in the world.

There is nothing more quintessentially human than sharing a story. Before there were books or churches, there were human communities that had to figure out how to survive in a dangerous and uncertain world. Humans weren't as fast as the antelope, as strong as the elephant, or as sharp-toothed as the lion. Their special gift and skill was the ability to care for each other and work together—to build community. And they did this through the magic of language and story.

In spite of those early childhood memories, many of us often wonder why it is that we don't simply act *rationally* to solve our problems. It's because any rational act is always performed in context—the unspoken, unseen story that lies behind our actions. If we have a story that tells us we are radically separate from the Earth, and from other people, and that our purpose is disembodied, individual salvation, it *is* rational to ignore the impact of climate change; it *is* rational for a society to have extreme—and growing—economic disparities; it *is* rational to think of our struggles as our own rather than part of the same collective struggle.

Modernity—the worldview that is based on the story I have referred to as the cosmology of loneliness—is rooted in the emergence of colonialism and capitalism. In these systems, lines were drawn—both in maps and in the human imagination—to separate that which is valued or sacred from that which is considered a mere resource. Even other human beings could be exploited or enslaved in such a system. Forests were razed, lakes and rivers redirected and poisoned. The Protestant Reformation in the sixteenth century put an increased importance on the salvation of the individual and taught that prosperity was a sign of God's favor: What did it matter if we destroyed the Earth if we were just trying to leave it all behind to get into heaven anyway? We couldn't be blamed for exploiting workers if this was merely God's will, a sign of our favor and their condemnation, could we? Many human beings gained a great deal of wealth and advanced technologically during this period, but it came at a great cost. We lost our place in the world.

While the notion of seeing a more interconnected world may seem radical, it is consistent with human cultures throughout most of history. All cultures have shared stories—myths—that reveal their core assumptions and values and help place the individual in relationship to the community, including the non-human, ecological community. For millennia, small groups of humans lived in a story that allowed them to understand themselves as interrelated to their world and embedded in a web of ecological and social relationships. But things have changed.

THE COSMOLOGY OF LONELINESS AND EDUCATION FOR LIBERATION

I will use the term cosmology synonymously with worldview, a way to describe how basic assumptions about the order of the world and our place in it, brought forth by cultural narratives. Cosmic loneliness is the result of a narrative that advocates for radical, absolute individualism. It isn't merely the product of being alone; it is the way we experience the world when our worldview is rooted in a story that tells us we are fundamentally separate from others, when we privilege independence over interdependence and relationship. How does this actually look in the world? In other words, how is the world put together through this story? Let's look at a few different elements of human experience.

1. *The Political.* "Totalitarian movements are mass organizations of atomized, isolated individuals," writes Hannah Arendt in *The Origins of Totalitarianism.* The political landscape today is dominated by the reality of our arrival at the precipice, the edge of our world. Indeed, we are in the midst of falling off the cliff of an old story, a cosmo-vision that organized our world for the last 500 years, a story called Modernity. Our choice is stark: we can attempt to cling to the imagined past, reaching for the ever-receding cliff—this choice is called fascism, a political system that focuses on power,

nationalism, and conservative values—or embrace a new vision.

2. *The Economic.* The capitalist system feeds and is fed by loneliness. Lonely people need to buy what they are selling; for it is through our sense of ourselves as isolated individuals that we have the need to consume infinitely, and this is what the system requires.
3. *The Ecological.* Our sense of ourselves as disconnected from the ecological web of life is part and parcel of the cosmology of loneliness.
4. *The Social.* Our social interactions have become increasingly mediated, and decreasingly organic. The paradox of social media as that while we have increased our capacity to connect on a superficial level, we have become increasingly isolated and lonely.

So how did we get here? How did we end up seeing ourselves as alone rather than part of the interconnected web of life, in spite of what we know from modern science and in spite of what we have always known in the cosmologies of every traditional culture on the planet?

I use the word "education" in its broadest sense here, in that it is simply the way in which a culture conveys to its young people who they are, why they are, and where they might seek to go. In this way, our current approach to education reinforces the cosmology of loneliness through its very structure, its processes, its *stories.*

To understand how this happens in the Modern classroom, it is useful to understand the metaphors of modern education—the fundamental stories and symbols through which we understand our world and upon which the structure of the classroom is based. The relationship between world and classroom is recursive: the cultural narratives that shape our world determine the shape of the classroom;

in turn, the classroom's core metaphors shape the world our children will create. I believe that our schools are based upon three metaphors that guide our civilization.

1. *The Factory*. Arising out of the industrial revolution, Modern schools are designed like factories, conceiving of the student as a product. Our students move from class to class, a little of each subject deposited in them—empty vessels—for a precise amount of time. The mechanistic nature of the school gives rise to a world conceived of as a machine.
2. *The Prison*. This is perhaps most obvious among marginalized youth, for whom the emphasis is on the punitive rather than the restorative. The idea here is that the child is fundamentally flawed and must be disciplined into success. The school and the community in which it is placed are something to be escaped. In addition to the obvious racist and classist overtones at play here, there are also subtle Christian undertones rooted in the Augustinian Fall. The world is fallen and flawed, as is the human. It is something to be escaped.
3. *The Free Market*. More recently, the notion that our schools ought to run according to the principles of free market capitalism has become increasingly popular. School districts are run by "CEOs"—often technocrats rather than educators—rather than superintendents. In programs like "Race to the Top" they are pitted against one another, competing for resources. And individual students in the classroom are pitted against one another, competitors rather than collaborators. This metaphor affects the curriculum as well. Rather than a liberatory curriculum, or at least one that helps a child grow into an adult capable of participating in the democratic process, our curricula are increasingly

driven by the market and seek to foster skills and knowledge in order to compete in the global economy.

One will notice that with all three narratives, individuals are emphasized over relationships. Each is a deficit narrative, a story that emphasizes what the child lacks, rather than an asset narrative, emphasizing the gifts and wisdom that each child brings. At moments of crisis, we require not merely to know the stories of the culture; we require a pedagogy that reimagines these stories. In the next chapter, I offer alternative metaphors for classrooms that are organic and relational, fostering liberatory and asset-based pedagogies.

EDUCATION

Years ago, I traveled around the world, across Asia overland, through north Africa and Europe, and back to Chicago. I learned many things along the way—indeed, I encountered the poverty, the polluted air, and shrinking resources I refer to in this book—but perhaps more than anything I learned the reality of the singularity of this planet, an island from which we cannot escape. Choices made by wealthy countries on one side of the planet were determining the lives of poor children on the other. We are stuck with each other, in this immense planet we cannot escape.

After my trip around the world, I went back to school, studying the world's great mystical and mythological traditions. But I couldn't seem to get away from my roots as an educator on the margins. While in school in California, I teamed up with a teacher to co-create a program for teens. I had learned from my travels and from my studies that the world's wisdom traditions all told their deepest truths not in lists of rules but in their stories. I also saw that the stories young people had about themselves were often their biggest impediment. For example, young people who dropped out of school or got arrested were always taught that this was simply because of their "poor choices." And surely there is some truth to that. But only in a worldview that isolates the individual as radically as ours could we reach the conclusion that anyone's life was *only* the product of personal choice. We are interconnected; our stories are woven together. When an adolescent gets in trouble, the story is far more complex than individual choice. The individual is a web of relationships. A young person who drops out of school didn't *choose* an inequitable society, a dysfunctional family, or a failing school system.

The high school dropout didn't choose that any more than we choose climate change, or the shrinking of the middle class. But somehow, we tend to blame those on the margins for their own marginalization while absolving the richest and greediest who are causing so much destruction. We refer condescendingly to certain kids as "at-risk," but what of our at-risk planet, our at-risk species? Indeed, the notion that consumer choice would be the solution to climate change is based on a false premise, radical individualism. But not only is it not the solution, it's actually a major cause.

While surely there are those who have good intentions when they try to push consumers toward more sustainable choices, just as educators mean well when they try to get their most at-risk students to make good choices. But the fetish of individual choice is rooted in the story behind the capitalist system, and this is the system that is causing both the climate crisis and social inequity in the first place. We *all* need a new story, not just those on the margins. This isn't about blame; it's about a story that can help us all find our place and recognize that we are not really alone, but that we are in this together, on this single planet.

In 2009, I moved to Chicago and started the Chicago Wisdom Project, a program to work with youth on the south side of Chicago. Over time, we developed a process that gave our young people the tools to reimagine their stories. This process isn't just healing for the participant. It also transforms the student into a teacher. The practices that the reader will find within this book have been developed in this process in dialogue with intellectual and academic ideas. They come forth out of the work that our teachers—including me—have done together with students. Sometimes the ideas we have had didn't exactly work out the way we expected. And that's okay. A curriculum ought not be created in the abstract, but co-created with the intrinsic imagination of the classroom. Over time, as we grew and merged with the Baltimore Wisdom Project to form Wisdom Projects, Inc., these ideas have continued to evolve. New practices, new ideas, new stories have emerged as students and teachers learn together.

The stories we tell offer new ways of seeing the world. That's why it's especially important that our stories come from multiple points of view, especially from those at the margins. There is a wisdom there that simply won't be found by those at the centers of power, from those who benefit from our current systems.

But before we can reimagine a story, it's helpful to return to the lessons learned from an example of a learning space that is in many ways the opposite of the modern classrooms that promote the modern story of individualism—the one-room schoolhouse. To understand what that might be, we don't need to look at the curriculum. Rather, we need to imagine how the learning process would unfold in this space.

I often invite people to visualize what they think of when they hear the word "classroom." Usually, it is some version of rows of desks with a teacher in the front. If it is a high school classroom, there will be a bell to alert them to move on to the next classroom. But when I ask what it means to be "educated" or about the times during which they learned the most, seldom is this narrow vision of the classroom involved: they are often outside, creating something, exploring the world, working together in community. Tellingly, when I ask people when they've felt most alive, or most fully human, the answers are similar. The work is to get the classroom to become the context for learning, for being alive and fully human.

Any classroom is a metaphor for the world. It can teach us the world is hierarchical and rigidly ordered; it can teach that the world is fluid, open, evolving. The classroom teaches us about our relationship to power, to our own agency, to our place in community. In the schools most of us attended, we learned that the world was something like the factories on which our public school system was modeled. We learned that we are essentially individuals, competing with one another. This is the context in which the high school dropout is blamed for "poor choices." But the one-room schoolhouse was a community. It had to be. The older students must teach the younger. Students and teachers must learn to get along. They were stuck with each other, in this little world they cannot escape.

It is easy to conceive how we might fall in love with a small community that shares a history and a culture rooted in local ecology and shared stories. But our challenge now is planetary. The Earth is a lot bigger and more diverse than the one-room schoolhouse or an isolated culture that inhabits an island. But the Earth is also, in some ways, both schoolhouse and island. How can we tell a story that connects us on a planetary scale?

In this book, you'll find a process to empower our young people to reimagine basic assumptions about the world—their story. It is our current story—the story of separation and individualism—that makes us lonely. While I cannot promise an easy solution to every crisis that a community or individual might encounter, I *can* promise that the solution will be found only if we face our fears and overcome our loneliness. Stories are necessarily created and shared in community; and joy is cultivated in community and intimacy. This can be with other human beings or with non-humans. Joy is the opposite of, the antidote to, loneliness. And even if our species doesn't survive, wouldn't we want to live more joyfully? Finding joy in such times requires genuine courage.

With a new story, we can begin to see our world, and our crises, in a new, healthy, and holistic way. Moreover, we can work through our personal trauma and loneliness. The new story will put us in context, in relationship, showing us that we are truly in this together. It is then that we can become teachers and leaders in this movement not merely to survive, but to thrive on the Earth. This is easier said than done. It's crucial that we have the right values and context for the new story to emerge.

While we must begin to think globally, we also must act not only locally, but in ways that align with our specific gifts and purpose. Moreover, reducing our problems to legality or politics and personal shopping habits draws a line between other actions that can be just as important. Loneliness is a holistic problem, for it has to do with our lack of relationship; its solutions, therefore, are found in many ways we might find surprising. We need activists, sure. But we also need better parents and teachers; we need thriving, egalitarian democracies. All this is the ultimate work of education.

***

My hope is that this book offers a pathway to the points above. For many readers, these points will challenge some basic assumptions about our place in the world. For example, one of the basic assumptions this new story must challenge is the notion that our inner lives and our outer problems are separate. "What happens to the outer world happens to the inner world," writes Thomas Berry (1999). "If the outer world is diminished in its grandeur then the emotional, imaginative, intellectual, and spiritual life of the human is diminished or extinguished. Without the soaring birds, the great forests, the sounds and coloration of the insects, the free-flowing streams, the flowering fields, the sight of the clouds by day and the stars at night, we become impoverished in all that makes us human." The seven principles in the next chapter offer approaches to recognizing that we are never truly alone, that we already have access to community in some form, and that we cannot separate our inner and outer lives.

All this is to say that our crisis is an educational one. But only in the very broadest sense. This isn't merely about what happens in schools. It is about how the cosmos itself is the very context for learning, and about how we learn to live and grow and learn together in community.

What I cannot promise in this book is a clear vision for what lies beyond. Like the earliest humans sitting around the fire, we are putting together a new world in story and symbol in order to survive and thrive in uncertain times.

Our Paleolithic ancestors can teach us something else, too. The ancient shamans of early human cultures climbed deep into the caves in which they lived and drew on the walls. The images of the cave paintings tell us so much about their world, their minds, their stories. First, they drew the images of predator and prey, the other living creatures on whom their survival depended. They understood deeply—not scientifically, but as part of their shared story—how interrelated they were to other living beings. The images they drew were reflections of the night sky and the constellations they perceived through both imagination and observation, an intersection of their interior lives and the cosmos itself.

The other image on the walls of the cave was the handprint. I can remember, still, when my wife was pregnant with our first child, seeing the little hand pushing out on the edge of the womb, her world. I remembered the caves at Altamira that I'd visited years before. I realized then that these ancient shamans saw themselves in the womb of the Earth, ready to be born. They, like us, like my unborn daughter, couldn't possibly have imagined what was coming next.

These caves can be thought of as the first classrooms, at once the human soul and cosmos, a space for inner work and creative expression. For the earliest humans, the microcosm represented a story that represented their world. So what does the classroom of today's world look like? What are the values of our new world and what is our place in it? It is with consideration of this question that we begin the next chapter.

Chapter 2

The Context for Education

The One-Planet Classroom

To say that our crisis requires new kinds of educating does not merely mean that we need to teach new or better content. Surely, there are new skills and knowledge required for this new world that is emerging. But how, precisely, does one prepare for a world so radically different? Before we can even discuss the learning process, we must think about the space in which we are learning. For it is the space that offers the metaphor for the world.

Let us remember how the one-room schoolhouse functions. While one-room schoolhouses surely aren't perfect, they understand exactly the function they serve: a learning context—a little world—that is an expression of values.

The most important question one can ask, therefore, at this moment of planetary crisis is what are the values that ought to shape a classroom at this moment? What are the principles that ought to guide us to deal with the crisis—inner and outer; ecological, political, economic?

It is curious that many of our institutions often invest so much into shaping a classroom without ever really asking why. In other words, we invest a great deal of time and money into desks, computers, buildings. But have we ever considered the lessons that are taught with those materials and the way they are arranged? We have doubled down, as it were, on patterns of movement and communication—lining up for recess, raising hands to speak—without ever considering how those patterns will be played out in the world beyond the school.

As you may notice, this isn't really about a classroom or about a school in the conventional sense. It's about how to construct a little world, a microcosm of the world we hope to create. In this sense, this chapter represents both the beginning and end of a recursive learning process. We begin with a classroom shaped by these principles (microcosm) and hope to end with a world shaped by them (macrocosm).

With this in mind, I offer a set of principles, metaphors, if you will, for the values of the world we hope to create. Each example will provide the values that will inform how learning spaces are structured.

THE WHOLE: CULTIVATING PLANETARY CONSCIOUSNESS

> *By the sole fact of his entering into 'Thought,' man represents something entirely singular and absolutely unique in the field of our experience. On a single planet, there could not be more than one centre of emergence for reflexion.*
>
> – Pierre Teilhard de Chardin (de Chardin 1965, p. 225)

The shape of the classroom is a sphere, an island floating in space, and is as vast as the human imagination.

A culture always creates a holistic vision of cosmos, community, and self. Through symbol and story, a narrative comes together that tells us how we came to be and how we belong. The context for this vision changes, but the holistic nature of it does not. The scope of this vision may be smaller, but it is always a vision for the entire cosmos. This is how worlds are made.

Each vision is, as long as it is fully developed and integrated into the culture, equally accurate, holistic, and cosmic.

But wait, you might ask, how is the vision of an uncontacted tribe in the Amazon or an isolated island in the Pacific as all-encompassing as the 13.7 billion year vision of modern science?

Let's begin with the notion of "accuracy." The best measure of a cosmology's "accuracy" (I use the scare quotes because such language reflects the overvaluing of the quantitative in our culture, and a standard that is poorly applied to other cultures) is in how it helps to cultivate meaningful, sustainable relationships in its context. The context is the whole. For an uncontacted Amazonian tribe, their context is the area of the forest in which they live. There is a story that tells them their place in that story and, if it is a functioning culture, how they can live meaningful, ordered, and sustainable lives. For most of human history, the context for cultural narratives would have been fairly similar to those of the uncontacted Amazonians.

Imperial cultures brought with them the first cosmopolitan worldviews. These had their problems. In many cases, narratives were constructed to reinforce the power imbalances of such societies. But in what later came to be known as the Axial Age, religious traditions emerged that allowed for the individual to connect to find a place in the world beyond the immediate clan and ecosystem. The evolution of the Israelite and Hindu traditions is particularly informative here.

With the destruction of the Second Temple and expulsion of the Jewish people from Palestine, a new form of Judaism emerged that was no longer based on the centrality of the Temple in Jerusalem or the priesthood. The Rabbi was a mere teacher whose role was to bring the Torah to the people. Israel's temple was found wherever Jews could gather.

Vedic Hinduism, also focused on temple sacrifice, developed new forms of spirituality known as Vedanta. Vedantic Hinduism, most notably in the writings of the Upanishads, focused not on the hierarchy of caste and of temple rituals but on the interiorization of the absolute—the *atman* or absolute self related to the absolute divine or cosmic. The fires of the sacrifice or *tapas* were the heating of one's own internal fire. The seven cosmic spheres were now the seven *chakras* within the human body.

Despite the universality and cosmopolitanism of the Axial traditions, there is still something missing. The paradox that lies at the heart of religion and nature—and this is the question we are indeed grappling with right now—is how to retain a sense of our connection to the world around us, the world we can touch and feel and taste and to the world and planet as a whole. This is, in many ways, the challenge that climate change has presented. Our cosmos is the planet now, and we must consider the spaces in which we teach and learn and grow together as metaphors for the Earth as a whole.

So, the aim is to bring forth a narrative, a set of symbols, that give rise to the sense of the planet as our basic context—our *home*. In other words, in the broadening of our world, those of us who have abandoned indigenous cosmologies for cosmologies of dualism (imagining of our interior, spiritual lives to be separate from the world) or loneliness now must uncover a cosmology in which the Earth is the context for our process of discovery.

The Classroom

What would learning spaces look like that fostered planetary consciousness and considered the Earth to be its basic context? To begin with, such a classroom might not be a classroom at all; for such a consciousness requires us to connect with the *immensity* if our world. We must walk outside and experience the Earth's curvature over the sea, the vastness of space. In the early days of running the Chicago Wisdom Project, we began to take our students to rural Michigan for weekend retreats. It was there, for the first time, that many of our students saw the stars. They were in awe. But this isn't merely about immensity; it's also about *intimacy*. Yes, our world is unfathomably vast and we are unimaginably small; but we can also recognize that we are in relationship to this vast world, and find intimacy and connection.

There are significant practical barriers to learning in this way. Many young people don't have open spaces; many teachers feel confined to the classroom. But there are things we can do to foster planetary consciousness in the classroom. To begin, classrooms must be multicultural spaces that avoid sectarian symbols—think of a globe rather than a flag. Multiple languages must be spoken; rituals must be drawn from various cultures.

Moreover, the context for learning must be expressed through the timeline of Big History—the story of the Universe—and through maps and globes that situates the student in relation to the whole. In other words, through space and time, we must create a learning environment that contextualizes everything with the whole.

The World

The world we hope to bring forth is one in which we understand the interconnectivity of it and that there are global challenges that cannot be addressed with narrow and parochial interests. This requires an imaginative leap—we simply have not evolved to conceptualize problems of a planetary scale. To imagine that world, we must foster an understanding of this broader, planetary context.

There are, of course, many ways in which we must return to the local, where the fetish of globalization has become toxic. But the hyper local, or parochial, can be toxic, too. Let's take the problem commonly referred to as the "migrant crisis." When we think of this as an issue of "border control," we've reduced a global problem to its localized expression and reified the artificial construct of a border. For the problems that bring migrants to a border do not honor borders. The migrant arrives at the border because of an interconnected system linking geopolitics, economics, and climate. A border is an expression of toxically localized consciousness. Whether a person becomes a refugee because of war, economy, or climate, the problems of the migrant crisis cannot be solved with this level of awareness.

DEPTH: THE THIRD DIMENSION

I want to know what happened to Icarus

after his wings melted away,

When he fell into the fathomless sea.

This is where the story begins.

The shape of the classroom is three-dimensional, engaging in the interior as well is the exterior.

The shift of our species into screen worlds is perhaps the most dramatic experiment in history with human consciousness. In a generation, we've gone from talking to each other, touching one another, to largely interacting with the world through a screen.

It wasn't so long ago that we were hearing about how the uprisings known as the Arab Spring were all because of Facebook. Somehow, we were told, Facebook allowed people to connect to one another in ways that they never could have before. I was skeptical: no one ever explained how every other uprising in the history of the world had happened without Facebook. We were simply expected to accept this hypothesis as evidence of the glorious march of human technological progress. Social media was going to be a force for justice and truth, we were told.

A few years later, this theory unraveled spectacularly as it became clear that the internet in general, and social media platforms specifically, were spreading misinformation and fomenting the spread of fascist and racist ideas at an alarming rate. It allowed for the ascension of Donald Trump and other fascist movements around the world, from India to France to Brazil.

There's nothing inherently wrong with the technologies that enable this. Indeed, technologies are generally morally neutral. I wouldn't want to give up on, say, eyeglasses or bicycles. Other technologies are more ambiguous; specifically, we have created a culture in which our social and professional interactions are largely mediated by screens. This is the world that our remote learner currently occupies.

As with all technologies, there are, of course, appropriate uses for screen-based technologies. I've taught through Zoom a great deal, and I've found that, for a limited time, wonderful discussions can be had, particularly in higher education. But there is always something lost, especially for younger people. Living in sterile, two-dimensional spaces impoverish us. For such spaces make it too easy to look away from that which makes us uncomfortable, from the suffering and sorrow that are a part of life. It inhibits our ability to communicate through human touch and the nuances of body language. We miss out on the beauty and spontaneity and joy of the world that happens when we share space.

This is what I call the "texture" of the world. Its flattening reduces us to consumers, products, and algorithms. There is some psychological sense of security in all this. We can project a simplified version of ourselves on our social media profiles, one that has none of the messiness of our textured world. It is a flattened version of our world, one that elides the world's messiness, its suffering. It promotes that dulling of our senses and emotions. All this also obscures much of the beauty and joy in our world. And, perhaps most damning, it prevents our young people from facing themselves and the world's gravest challenges.

The Classroom

So, our learning spaces must be three-dimensional. That is, they cannot merely focus on concise skills and knowledge, but on our own emotional depth and on interiority. In this sense, a "classroom" is beyond what one can see. I want to be clear that when I speak of depth and the classroom: I am suggesting that the interiority of each child is as much a part of the learning space as the tables and chairs and books.

This means that the classroom must contain processes that emphasize the often unseen and unspoken social and emotional aspect of growth and development. Such processes aren't merely add-ons or put into place when there is a problem; they are woven into every subject, every activity.

The World

The three-dimensional world that is brought forth from educating our children in this way is one in which we can be more present. In other words, rather than primarily inhabiting the shallow, two-dimensional spaces of our screen-centered world, we become present to the world in all its messiness and chaos.

Moreover, creating a learning environment that includes the depth and interiority of self and others leads us into an adulthood in which we are aware of the emotional lives of others and ourselves. This sounds simple, but our world needs more people who know how to love, who know how to cry.

DIFFERENCE AND DIVERSITY

> *The best way to know God is to love many things.*
>
> – Vincent Van Gogh (in Edwards 1989, p. 69)

The shapes of the classroom are infinite.

It is easy to glorify the concept of our shrinking planet. More connected than ever, the thinking goes, we will understand one another better. In the West, there is a belief that democracy and human rights are being spread through some combination of the internet and capitalism—with a little bit of military thrown in.

But the emergence of a single planetary culture has a shadow side as well. In my travels around the world, I have come to see that the beauty of such journeys is found partly in its complexity, its variety. That isn't to say there aren't things one finds in common throughout humanity. But there is a difference between what I might uncover as a universal human quality and the imposition of a global monoculture. All around the world, English is spoken—and it is no coincidence that American dollars are used along with this. As languages die, worldviews die. Unique and beautiful cultures die.

Another time, I taught English in rural Zimbabwe. There, I discovered our purpose was partly altruistic, but also part of a process to bring people into the global capitalist order. We taught them English, but even more insidiously, we taught them to function on a schedule. It became apparent that this was more important in development aid than teaching academics. For scheduling—in other words, buying and selling abstract time—is a key to entering the global capitalist order.

There is a parallel between biodiversity and cultural diversity. A healthy ecosystem is diverse because each species requires other niches to be filled to have balance. For example, the predator cannot live without prey. What's more, there are myriad microorganisms that recycle and reproduce healthy air and soil. While we might fear the wolf or be annoyed by the fly, those species benefit the whole, and benefit us. Indeed, our collapsing biosphere is largely the result of a loss of biodiversity. Similarly, an individual species requires genetic diversity. When a new disease is introduced, the species has a better chance of surviving if it is genetically diverse.

Cultural diversity serves a similar purpose. If the only culture valued is that of Western Capitalism, how can we find new ways of seeing the world when it becomes apparent—as is surely the case now—that a new worldview is required? Indeed, a large part of our difficulty in seeing beyond market- and consumption-based solutions to climate change is the fact that our discourse is so dominated by this single story. Diversity—whether it is of people, cultures, or ideas—is inherently more democratic and less hierarchical. And it can be revolutionary in that it allows for the ideas that come from the margins, not just Wall Street or the ivory tower, to be heard.

The Classroom

Whereas the modern, traditional classroom typically has a focal point, a central figure or purpose, let's imagine a classroom with multiple centers and shared leadership. We learn, in such a space, that the world is multi-perspectival. For example, someone who thrives in one context may need help in another; those who might be considered "at risk," can have much to share and teach if they can find the proper context to access their gifts.

A learning space that is shaped physically with multiple centers can also be a space for a diversity of ideas.[1] We are confronted with challenges that are largely caused by our conventional patterns of thought—for example, the belief that we are separate from nature and that we must manage and control it—and, therefore, the solutions require new patterns and ideas. To do so, it requires us to recognize that everyone brings a unique and valuable perspective. For example, a teacher may have a master's degree, and that knowledge and experience is valuable and should be honored by the student. But a student may also bring a range of experiences—a veritable PhD in their own life—that should also be honored.

Lastly, everyone is diverse in that they possess a range of qualities that make up a whole person. As described in the next chapter, a complete learning process involves each aspect of the human, not just the intellectual. Moreover, getting to know oneself involves a recognition of this internal diversity, even when we are confronted with contradictions. The Self can at once embody contradictory elements; embracing the paradoxical nature of our selves is a pathway to self-acceptance and -compassion and compassion for others.

The World

As we are confronted with collapsing ecosystems worldwide, it is clear that biodiversity is essential for our survival. A thriving ecosystem requires a variety of species to fill various niches. We are culturally programmed to think in terms of hierarchies rather than webs, but the reality of an ecosystem is that it can only be understood and can only flourish with diversity. The bacterium and the insect are just as important as the human. The apex predator is essential. There are no good guys and bad guys. But we've dramatically reduced our world's biodiversity, and the planet is in peril because of it. At the same time, we have also reduced the genetic diversity of many species, from apple trees to cattle, through selective breeding. When this happens, a species is less likely to survive disease.

Educators can similarly affect cultural diversity. When we are limited in our ways of thinking, we are less likely to find novel solutions to our problems. The global monoculture, spread through colonialism and capitalism, has pressured people worldwide to conform to a particular cultural norm. Thousands of human languages have died, each representing a unique way of experiencing the world, a cosmovision from which, perhaps, we could learn something.

Lastly, just as it is mentally healthy to accept our personal internal contradictions, and to accept them in others, we all must learn to accept the paradoxical nature of the world, to embrace the world's diversity.

ECOLOGY

> *A human being is a part of the whole called by us universe, a part limited in time and space. He experiences himself, his thoughts and feeling as something separated from the rest, a kind of optical delusion of his conscious-*

ness. This delusion is a kind of prison for us, restricting us to our personal desires and to affection for a few persons nearest to us. Our task must be to free ourselves from this prison by widening our circle of compassion to embrace all living creatures and the whole of nature in its beauty.

– Albert Einstein (in Cohen 2003, p. 83)

The shape of the classroom is a web.

Capitalist ideology teaches that the individual is the basic context of human culture. When humans get together, they do so as individuals choosing to do so. Classrooms and cultures are, therefore, spaces of conflict and competition. Our relationship to the non-human world is erased in this approach to learning. We are educated, generally, to navigate human institutions.

An ecological classroom would shift the emphasis from human individuals to relationships, and from the exclusively human to the web of life. And, of course, this sensibility extends beyond the realm of human relationships into that which is literally ecological. Ecology is the study of life in relationship and how it interrelates as a holistic system. Literally, it means "home." And it is the basic context for the human, how we came into being in relationship.

Evolution is inseparable from the study of ecology, its temporal dimension. Whereas the physical context for the ecological classroom is the web of relationships, the temporal context is the story of the universe. Each moment in this story represents not merely a scientific fact, but also an ancestor, a part of who we are.

Buddhist philosophy is informative here. In the Buddhist worldview, the individual is understood to be "empty." This doesn't mean that one doesn't exist; it means that the self is fundamentally in *relationship*. We cannot pinpoint or isolate the self without including the web of relationships and actions that connect us. We are interdependent. There is an ethical component to interdependence. If I can see that my self is not actually separate from others, I can be compassionate, recognizing that my own well-being is entangled in everyone else's.

Deep ecology extends ecology beyond superficial relationships and holds that we can shift our consciousness and cultural practices toward natural relational networks. In other words, ecology can refer not merely to the science of the ecosystem, but also to the inner- and cultural life of the human. We are, after all, enmeshed in the ecosystem just as much as the bacterium or the wolf. In creating an ecological classroom—beyond simply learning *about* ecology—we can foster this kind of consciousness.

The Classroom

The ecological classroom is rooted in relationship and attention to the non-human, living world. In simple terms, this means getting outside and getting in touch with the local ecology and bioregion. Just as the conception behind the classroom of "planetary consciousness" encouraged a connection to the entire planet and the vastness of the cosmos, the point here is to find a connection to the local. Whether inside or outside, the classroom can reflect the specific species and biorhythms of the local bioregion.

Moreover, an ecological sensibility is centered on *relationship*. This is also the foundation of restorative practices.[2] When there is a conflict, the restorative classroom focuses primarily on restoring relationships rather than on seeking retribution for particular individuals.

In its emphasis on relationship, the ecological classroom isn't merely outside or focused on nature—although these things can and should be a part of any curriculum. Indeed, any process can be ecological insofar as it fosters an ecological sensibility through our interactions and learning processes. We are nature, and, therefore, human relationships are inherently ecological. This means that we can relate to one another systemically—that is, our problems and conflicts can be solved by restoring relationships; the work of the classroom can be done collaboratively, with students as partners rather than rivals.

An important aspect of ecology is that there is no "outside." It is primarily from the relationships *within* the learning space that we learn. Sorting out disagreement and coming to an understanding of shared values is an important part of the learning process.

The World

The pan-African concept of *Ubuntu* describes a conception of being rooted in community: "*A person is a person through people.*" It is, in a sense, an ecological sense of self. In an ecosystem, each is a unique expression of the whole, of the web of relationships that give rise to the individual. This can also be a way of understanding human social relationships. While I am unique, I am also deeply connected—interconnected—with others. But it's more than just the fact that I am in relationship; my very identity is inextricably linked to my community. This sense of self rooted in community is an ecological model for society. What if, instead of the self-interest advocated by capitalism, we valued interdependence and relationship?

In many ways, ecology represents the opposite approach to life from industrial capitalism. And while it is essential that we reimagine human relationships, of course, there is even more at stake here. Recognizing our place, our sense of home, in the web of ecological relationships—our connection to other living beings—is fundamental to our survival and to the flourishing of life on the planet. In an age of ecological crisis, the only way forward is ecological civilization; and this cannot even be envisioned without the ecological classroom.

THE POWER OF CIRCLES

Conversation is a game of circles

– Ralph Waldo Emerson

The power of the world always works in circles.

– Black Elk (Elk and Neihardt 2014, p. 121)

The shape of the classroom is a circle, wherein each person sees and hears each other.

The most basic decision a teacher and student must make is where to sit or stand. The classic image one thinks of in any classroom is that of children lined up in rows and a teacher standing in front. This structure is played and replayed in obvious and in more subtle ways throughout the school day, throughout our educational lives, and, most importantly, in our broader world.

The hierarchical classroom reinforces power relationships of hierarchical societies. In ceding their power to the teacher, students not only relinquish their own power, they also learn that the only way to be seen and heard is to put themselves in positions of power. The classroom, and the world, becomes a context for seeking this access, and for relentless competition.

If we could reimagine that classroom as a circle, or as a space in which to form multiple circles, we would see a learning space that fosters the notion that each person is of equal value, each person is seen and heard. Such a classroom is a metaphor for a world that is more consistent with the structure of human society for most of human history—the indigenous society. The hierarchical classroom is the product of imperial, industrial, capitalist society, wherein the values of hierarchy that first emerged with large, complex imperial society became automated and mechanized.

The Classroom

Our classroom is not merely a circle—it is a *sacred* circle. The circle is more than a way to arrange chairs, it also provides a container, a safe space in which learning, sharing, and exploration can take place. And so, we begin by recognizing that the classroom is a different kind of space, a ritualized space that requires a different kind of consciousness to enter.

The child's imagination already understands this. In any game, there is an unspoken agreement that we are entering into a space in which there are new rules, that the symbolic relationships contained within are different. A sport isn't unlike this. On the field or court, we agree upon a certain form of relationship and participation. When we exercise minds and bodies in this context, we become stronger.

But the agreement of the sacred circle is different from the agreement of sport. In the circle, each person can see the other; each must listen to the other. While of course the teacher may know things the student does not, each person in the circle is respected and heard and is of equal value.

More broadly, one can think of the classroom as part of a relational schema of concentric circles. The typical way of thinking about the individual and classroom relationship would be that the classroom is a container and the individual is inside that container along with others. In this case, however, we can envision the individual as the center of a series of concentric circles, each representing that individual's identity in a broader sense. The classroom, therefore, is not merely context, a space separate from the student;

rather, it is a part of who the student is. As we continue to move out with each concentric circle, we arrive at the world.

The World

As is the case with many of these metaphors, they are both about the world we want to create and about reflecting the world as it really is. Our world is more circular than linear. In nature, we find spirals and circles—certainly we seldom find straight lines. Indeed, even time is less linear than our clocks and schedules would have us think. So, perhaps, the notion of linear time and of rigid boundaries is more something we have projected onto the world rather than a reflection of the world as it is. In other words, it is due to the structure of our classrooms when the classroom's values are projected onto the broader world.

There are more than just ideas about the world at stake here. The circular classroom is a way to value everyone equally. This doesn't mean that each of us is the same and that those with more experience or skill cannot be honored and respected; it means that each of us is valued for our unique gifts and perspectives. It means that in a democracy, we do not allow those with more money to have undue influence and adhere to the principle of "one person, one vote."

Humility

If we surrendered
to earth's intelligence
we could rise up rooted, like trees.

Instead we entangle ourselves
in knots of our own making
and struggle, lonely and confused.

So like children, we begin again. . .

to fall,
patiently to trust our heaviness.
Even a bird has to do that
before he can fly.
– Rainer Maria Rilke (in Barrows and Macy 2005, p. 171)

The shape of the classroom is uncertain, cannot be prescribed, and emerges through intrinsic relationships.

What if we started the shape of our space with emptiness? As educators, what if we started our relationship to our students by saying, "I don't know?" In this way, we can begin a process of shared inquiry, of asking questions, of modeling epistemic humility—the value in knowing what one doesn't know.

The word "humility" shares a root with the word humus, or soil. It refers to being grounded, humble. *Earthy*. In this way, we are talking about the value of organic processes, rather than engineered ones; we are talking about the intrinsic creativity of the learning community itself rather than ideas imposed from the teacher, or worse, the bureaucrat.

The classroom, therefore, is *empty*. I mean this in the Buddhist, rather than the literal, sense. Its shape emerges from relationship and shared decision-making. The educator, therefore, can at once instill humility in the student by modeling it—always a better way to make a person humble than by constantly beating them down—and, at the same time, empower the student by allowing for the classroom and its processes to be shaped by them. In listening, the teacher teaches that the student also has something to teach.

The Classroom

This is more about what we don't do in the classroom than what we do. In other words, it asks us to think less in terms of designing a learning space than in fostering a sense of intrinsic creativity in which the learning space is co-created by students and teachers together.

Let's imagine that a classroom is empty the first time we enter it. Its symbols and decorations, even the way it is arranged, can be structured by the students through organic interactions. In this way, the classroom becomes a reflection of the intrinsic creativity of the world.

There is also a pedagogical element to the classroom of humility. And this has to do with the teacher's participation in the circle. The educator or leader of the classroom is not separate from the circle, but a participant with a unique role. They ask questions; they listen; they honor the stories of the students.

The World

The opposite of humility is hubris. And it is hubris that perhaps most defines the modern era in which we have consistently believed we can engineer our way out of any crisis, that human ingenuity is superior to the Earth's creativity—the intrinsic processes that have evolved over billions of years of evolution.

There are abundant examples of this. So often, we have sought to engineer the planet for it to conform to our sense of what is needed. This has always been humanity's way. But this approach has accelerated in the industrial age. We've built dams to manage ecosystems that have led to their destruction, created systems of agriculture to deplete soils, introduced invasive species, toxified aquifers, all in the name of progress. As we face perhaps our greatest challenges—climate change, mass extinction, ecological collapse—we again return to the very logic that got us here—that we can engineer our way out of every problem rather than shifting our approach from hubris to humility.

WILDNESS AND PLAY

> *A child who does not play is not a child, but the man who does not play has lost forever the child who lived in him.*
>
> – Pablo Neruda

> *We need the tonic of wildness . . . At the same time that we are earnest to explore and learn all things, we require that all things be mysterious and unexplorable. . . .*
>
> – Henry David Thoreau

The shape of the classroom is formless chaos.

Any parent will tell you that there is something scary about the fact that, no matter how hard we try to control them, our children will make their own choices. We can influence them, of course. We can give them punishments or rewards. But ultimately our children choose who they are. As older, more experienced people, we wish they'd just listen to our wisdom. We know something, after all, about the consequences of certain choices. But this is the beauty of childhood, too. For the child can see pathways and possibilities we cannot.

This fear is one of the driving forces of our approach to education. We so often choose control over freedom, the punitive over the liberatory. And this is because we fear the inherent wildness of the child. We fear it, in part, because we can perceive risks to the child's well-being better than the child can. But mostly we fear it because it brings about a loss of control. One cannot separate the racist and classist biases that exacerbate these fears. Wisdom Projects codirector Cleis Abeni (Upāsikā tree turtle) explains:

> The Black practitioners and activists within my network in the Consortium for Youth Services and Child Welfare like Brenda Strong Nixon, Anna Hall, Samuel H. Wilson, and Amos N. Wilson centered our work in anti-oppressive engagement. So often educators of Black youth become mired in implicit biases that make them focus almost entirely on scolding children by telling them how to behave in increasingly invigilating terms. Instead of only admonishing them by telling them how to behave, we believed in choosing our words very carefully when we speak with them. Careful phrasing and diction empowered them to behold the world with inquisitiveness and insightfulness, and not just behave. There is a direct relationship between the words that we use to engage with youth (and our tones of voice), and the way they feel when interacting with us. We did not abandon behavioral and classroom management. On the contrary, we believed fiercely in the need for elevating accountability in that work. Creating safe, respectful environments often demands clear advice about deportment and conduct. Yet, rather than only emphasizing behavioral management, we championed verbal expression typified by restorative practices that always humanized the youth through careful listening and sensitive elocution. For me, this listening, sensitive, and restorative engagement is the essence of cultural responsiveness (C. Abeni, personal communication).

Our children—especially children who have been marginalized—are too often told to behave, rather than behold.

The need for control is embedded into the collective psyche. More broadly, we've crafted a civilization rooted in a need for control. Indeed, civilization largely rests on the ability to control and manage—not just practically, but also emotionally—the wild and chaos of our natural world and the fear it elicits. The child is seen as part of this, not entirely civilized yet. And the unspoken purpose of school is to civilize our children.

We fear the wilderness—with good reason. For most of human history, the world beyond the womb of human culture and community was vast and dangerous. As a result, we've narrowed those wild areas to mere islands in the vast see of civilization, an inverse of what was historically true; we've killed off the big predators and the tiniest insects; we've even reduced the genetic diversity of produce and domesticated animals.

But in paving over so much of the world, we've also paved over something wild in ourselves.

The problem here is that wildness and play are the primary ways in which children learn. They take risks in their play, stretching their bodies and minds, exploring, and questioning the unknown. Indeed, this is how we learn and innovate as adults, too. Good scholarship is *play*; the arts are *play*; activism is *play*. We play when we invent something, create something, when we explore new ideas.

Moreover, planetary health requires wilderness and wildness. Indeed, while warming temperatures are obviously a threat to planetary health, so too is the loss of wilderness.

While there are practical, outcome-based reasons to integrate play into education, the element of *joy*, an outcome in itself, should not be minimized when we talk about play. Education ought not to be merely about solving problems or attaining certain outcomes. Perhaps the greatest purpose of childhood—and therefore of education—is joy. And play is the pathway to joy.

The Classroom

The learning space is play-based, child-centered, and, if possible, in wild spaces.

We begin with the child rather than the adult, because this is where we find less need to control, manage, engineer. The child's intuition pulls us toward play. And it is important to recognize that it is through play that most genuine learning happens. When we play, we are taking risks safely, stretching our bodies and minds, asking questions of our world and ourselves.

And while it isn't always possible, learning in wilderness or natural spaces can often foster this kind of free play and exploration. A forest can be a classroom just as well as a room in a building, and often a better one. Playing in nature fosters a love and respect for the wildness of the world and ourselves that is often absent in how we bring up our children.

The World

Our planet is dependent upon wilderness. A world in which wild spaces are protected is not only more sustainable, more ecologically diverse, less prone to pandemics and extreme weather—such a world is more beautiful, more mysterious. The human imagination has always required the beauty of the night sky, the forests, the deserts, the grasslands.

The human is an expression of the wildness of nature. And it is this spirit of wildness and play that also can help us find solutions to our problems, to innovate, to imagine a new world. So, human imagination requires wilderness and wildness as a context, and the sustenance of wild spaces requires human beings who are capable of thinking playfully, wildly, and joyfully.

NOTES

1. I want to be careful about how I frame this; for the notion of diversity has, at times, been used as an excuse to promote ideas that are, for example, racist or sexist. In the next chapter, we'll explore how a genuine intellectual inquiry can foster discernment. That fact that we require a diversity of ideas does not mean all ideas are equally valid.

2. I prefer this terminology to the more common "restorative justice" because it emphasizes that such principles, although surely appropriate to mediate conflict, can and should be used throughout the learning process (see Chapter 8).

Chapter 3

The Process for Education

A Pedagogy for Reimagining the Story

Whereas the previous chapter focused on the creation of space and the metaphors upon which that space is based, this chapter will focus on the process as we move through time—in other words, this is an exploration of how we engage one another and the practices and principles involved.

Just as some approaches to education have neglected to focus on the power of the learning space, we've also often failed to sufficiently focus on pedagogy—not merely what is taught, but also *how* one teaches it. So, before we address *what* we teach in the next section, we must understand *how* we might teach, because it's in the process as much as in the content that the true lessons are learned.

At the core of this approach is a holistic understanding of the human. The process begins and ends with an interconnected notion of the person. We cannot be reduced to the isolated, individual, so we begin with a learning space that is rooted in community and conclude with an integration into an interconnected world. We learn in relationship. The ultimate purpose of education is not mere individual success; it is to integrate one's learning into the world and to bring forth a more just and compassionate world for everyone.

In between the microcosm and macrocosm of classroom and world is a holistic vision of the learner. Just as the human cannot be reduced to the mind, education cannot be reduced to mere facts and skills. We are not—to repudiate the Cartesian dualism that dominates Modern Western thinking—mere thinking beings. Our feelings are as significant as our thoughts; we are bodies and ecologies. Ultimately, we are co-creators of our world and, as humans, we do this with our stories.

Education, therefore, is also a question of the story we tell. At this moment, there is an opportunity and a necessity to reimagine our story—our basic understanding of our place in the world. This chapter offers a holistic framework that empowers our youth to reimagine their stories.

HOLISTIC EDUCATION

This section offers three different models for thinking about education holistically: the Creation Spirituality theological tradition; multiple intelligence theory from developmental psychology; and philosophical tradition known as integral theory.

Matthew Fox is a theologian, former priest, and educator who first introduced the notion of holistic education to me. In his work with graduate students in spirituality, Fox, recognizing that spirituality cannot be fully understand through a merely intellectual lens, developed a pedagogical method that involved the whole person. He later implemented this process with teens in Oakland, California. He framed his holistic approach to working with teens through what he calls the "10 Cs" (Fox 2006):

1. **Contemplation:** Contemplation is the first C because the lesson should begin with a specific healing practice of the class. Students should understand the basic meaning and purpose of contemplation and meditation, as well as the philosophy and cosmology underpinning the practice.
2. **Character & Chakra Development**: To see the interconnectedness, the contemplative practice should move right into a discussion of Character. Contemplative practice serves not only to find inner peace, but to cultivate one's character in facing the world. What are the attributes that make up a person's character? Begin with the students' ideas about what constitutes a whole person and good character.
3. **Cosmology & Ecology**: The human body, as discussed in the first two Cs, is not separate from the world, but part of an interconnected community of beings. The chakra system, as in many cultures, shows the human body as a microcosm of the Universe. (The Seven Chakras are paralleled by the seven cosmic spheres.)
4. **Chaos & Darkness:** Chaos provides the balance for Cosmos. Students should recognize the difference between opposites (e.g. good and evil) and the dynamic tension of concepts like chaos and cosmos (or *yin* and *yang*, which is particularly important if students are using a contemplative practice based on the Chinese system). It refers to "disorder" now, but also comes from a Greek word meaning "void" or emptiness.

5. **Compassion:** Students should understand the meaning of compassion. It literally means "to feel with" (Latin *com*=with/*pathos*=feel). This is different from feeling sorry for someone or even to do what one thinks is fair.
6. **Community**: In many ways, one's capacity for compassion has to do with how community is defined. At this stage, the students should simply define what their community is. Students should be encouraged to think of community in ways that move beyond physical proximity.
7. **Critical Consciousness & Judgment**: What does it mean to think critically? When we are given information, do we always accept it? Whom do we trust? Friends? Parents? Peers?
8. **Courage**: Compassion and Critical Consciousness doesn't do us much good without courage.
9. **Creativity**: Instead of being given information to learn, the students become teachers as they integrate lessons and experiences and express them in their own, unique way. It is also helpful to ask the students what creative talents and interests they bring to the program.
10. **Ceremony, Celebration, & Ritual**: What rituals do you have in your lives? Why is ritual important for people of every culture and how does it build community? What happens to a society that has lost its rituals?

The 10 Cs are tools for teachers and students to think holistically about themselves, their place in the world, and their education. They encourage us to ask, "What are the values that guide our choices about what and how to teach?" and "What makes up a whole human, a whole community, a whole world?" It is essential to think holistically about education.

Multiple intelligence theory, first developed by Harvard developmental psychologist Howard Gardner (2006), posits that there are many ways of being intelligent, not merely the logical and linguistic that most schools emphasize. His original seven included the following:

Linguistic-verbal: This is the intelligence of words and ideas, reading and writing. It is generally covered by the academy through the humanities. In this holistic model, it is what the Greeks would have called *mythos*, our ability to understand our world through myth or story.

Logical-mathematical: Always emphasized in our schools, this is the intelligence of numbers and logic (Greek *logos*). While obviously prominent in mathematics, it also refers to a type of thinking, the logical or rational, that can be applied to any subject.

Musical-rhythmic and harmonic: This is the intelligence of the music and song.

Visual-spatial: This applies to both visual artists and to those who make things.

Bodily-kinesthetic: This is how we learn with our bodies and through physical action.

Interpersonal: This is a form of emotional and social intelligence that refers to our relationships.

Intrapersonal: This is the form of emotional intelligence that refers to how we know ourselves and process emotions.

Later, Gardner added two more: the "naturalistic," which is the intelligence that applies to nature, farming, and other forms of connecting to the non-human world; and the existential, which is explored further in Chapter 6. He even suggested that one could add teaching-pedagogical intelligence.

Integral theory provides an all-encompassing vision, a simple yet comprehensive way of conceiving of the whole. Its value is in that it provides a holistic vision—inner and outer; individual and collective—that also accounts for the passage of time and evolution.

The vision of integral theory accounts for four quadrants of human experience:

> **"I":** The interior-individual is how we evolve in deeper subjectivity and wisdom as individuals. Developmentally, this demonstrates how an individual organism evolves from the simplest awareness to deeper subjectivity. In this classroom, this would be represented by addressing a child's inner life.
>
> **"We":** The interior-collective is where the cultures evolve. Just as individuals possess an interiority and subjectivity, so too do communities. For example, we might study the ideas and cosmologies of various cultures.
>
> **"It":** The exterior-individual is how we evolve as individuals physically.
>
> **"Its":** The exterior-collective is about systems—politics for example—and how the world evolves collectively.

Applying these quadrants to a curriculum can provide a way to visualize just how holistic we are. At times, efforts at holistic approaches, while surely comprehensive in that they involve a wide variety of subject matter and learning modalities, they may often have blind spots, and this model can help to ensure that we address the interior and exterior of subject matter, the individual and the collective. It also offers a way to think of everything as *process*.

The following steps are not necessarily linear. Rather, they can be seen as a way to engage questions, ideas, skills, or narratives *holistically*. This benefits different learning styles, not just among students but within each student.

These steps draw from the holistic models above, but they also come out of many years of practice in the classroom—which sometimes was a room, sometimes a forest, sometimes a basketball court. It is a process that was brought forth in relationship to young people and fellow educators. In other words, the process I describe in this book emerged through entering into a similar learning process myself. As educators, the following will ensure that we aren't just talking about something, but also working through it as a whole person and with whole community. The end of the process isn't really an end at all. Just as for me, my work as a student led me to become a teacher, which led me again to become a student. The aim of the process is to start over, with new teachers and new insights.

COMMUNITY: SHARING THE STORY (REIMAGINING THE CLASSROOM)

Among the most fundamental assumptions of our systems of education is that we learn primarily as *individuals*. This assumption is rooted in the cosmology of loneliness. Our thinking about individual and community has been heavily influenced by Thomas Hobbes's theory of the "social contract," in which we are primarily individuals, and a community is a collection of individuals coming together. This story—and we should emphasize the word *story* here—is reinforced through capitalism, in which individual self-interest is emphasized. Our classrooms are often rooted in this notion. Rather than communities, they can be contexts for conflict and competition.

In my experience, the most important element—in a sense, the prerequisite for all other learning—is creating a culture of care. When children care about one another, they lift each other up. They listen. They bear witness to one another's stories. This is the foundation of compassion.

By building community, we learn from each other and learn of the interconnectedness of our stories. What are the stories we've been given? What individual story does each of us bring about our place in the world? How are these stories connected to the larger stories? In each subject area and in each "class" we should collaborate and consider how our work affects the local and global communities.

Our pedagogical process begins with the formation of community, which is fundamentally what a classroom or learning space is—or should be. It is here that we establish our relationship to one another as understood through the metaphors in the previous chapter. The concept of the sacred circle is a helpful way to think of community. For it emphasizes the way in which each participant is equally valued and cared for. Moreover, rather than an individual entering into a contractual relationship, each participant is fundamentally relational; the circle is not merely a space to enter into, but an aspect of one's self.

The process of sharing one's story in community means that we honor what each individual can bring to the circle. We share and listen to one another's stories and learn from them. The pedagogy, therefore, begins not with information or skills or the establishment of rules; rather, it begins with inquiry, listening, and the formation of a culture of care.

In each subject area, the pedagogical process begins with the creation of a learning community—and this, not a room with four walls, is what a classroom actually is—rooted in the seven principles of Chapter 2. In doing so, we have a context for liberation, joy, and the sharing of the stories each person brings to the learning space. The educator's role here is to focus on the space itself and, of course, to listen.

But this isn't only about learning as a community. The exploration of any subject begins, in a sense, with an understanding of how each subject also functions as a community: science is the study of cosmic and ecological communities; the arts are fundamentally about relationships, shared stories; our inner work is about how we take care of one another spiritually; our work is how we take care of each other materially; and social studies and history, when understood as rooted in community, become justice work.

Practice, Process, Pedagogy

Community building is foundational to any subject or learning process. Some basic guidelines for the establishment of the space are as follows:

1. The space itself is profoundly important. Create a space for transformative work. This can mean many different things: A space outside can be around a fire or in a grove of trees. Inside, pay special attention to avoiding distractions and creating a womb-like, cave-like space.
2. Be sure there is a clear beginning and end to the process. This can be done with silence as well as with other methods (e.g. drumming). Open with silence. Be sure that the entire group is present and that all distractions are removed (e.g. people not in the circle interrupting; cell phones and the like).
3. Use a talking stick (or any other object that can be held to symbolize who is speaking). Everyone should understand that only the facilitator and the person with the stick should talk during this time.
4. Encourage youth to be brief and to speak from the heart. Model this in your own speech.

5. Encourage youth not to interrupt. Even if they are trying to helpful, it is important to allow others to speak and to simply be heard.
6. Employ active listening. Rather than try to provide solutions, reflect/repeat to the person what they have said.

Above all else, this is the time for the students to share their stories and listen to others' stories. While the process above allows for more organic forms of sharing, it's often helpful to give students a format to see what emerges. The idea is that each student brings a story about the world—who they are and their place in it. In the past, we've used the "I Am" poem—seven lines, each beginning with the words "I Am"—to elicit this kind of sharing. We've found that students often share far more than they would without prompts. And often the sharing yields surprises; we find, for example, that we cannot be reduced to one thing, that we all contain contradictory elements. The point here is to listen rather than critique. We are merely learning and listening; criticism and transformation will come later.

INTELLECT: CRITIQUING THE STORY

As discussed in Chapter 1, we have all been given a story, a narrative about our place in the world. In the Modern Western world, this is often the story of disconnection and loneliness. It is the fundamental narrative upon which the shape of the Modern classroom is based. To transform or reimagine this story, rigorous intellectual work is required.

It is worth noting that just because a pedagogy is holistic and not narrowly focused on rational thought does not mean that it ought to be anti-intellectual. The intellect is indeed a significant part of any learning process. Fostering critical, flexible, and creative thinkers is essential. But it is important to understand what one means by "intellect"—and what the intellect is not.

Too often, the easily tested and quantified serves as a proxy for intellectual rigor. But the fact that something is quantifiable doesn't necessarily make it a more rigorous measure. In fact, the measurable, in lacking nuance, can often be *less* intellectually rigorous than that which defies quantification. Indeed, failing to train our youth to work through complex and nuanced problems and ideas is a major reason for their lack of readiness for higher education, and it represents an abandoning of the role of our schools in preparing our youth to participate in a democracy.

Genuine intellectual growth occurs through dialogue and inquiry. It is not the conveyance of discrete facts or skills, or even ideas, but about the process of shared inquiry, the in-between spaces wherein ideas are wrestled with. This is true even with the written word—or any other art form for that matter. The word on the page is not planted into the empty vessel of the student; rather, it comes to life when the author's story or idea is integrated, processed, and debated.

The highest form of intellect is found when we engage in nuance and paradox, when we wrestle with information and ideas that can at once be true and yet are seemingly in contradiction. This is profoundly important in the student's developing sense of self. For example, the best examples of "I Am" poems—and this frequently comes out in their work—are those in which there is nuance and paradox. A person can be many things at once, even if those things are in contradiction; our world is many things at once, even if those things are in contradiction. A recognition of this truth represents a higher form of intellectual and personal growth.

The nuance of the poet and the paradox of the mystic are alternatives to fascism and fundamentalism. A thriving democracy isn't merely about voting; it is about how we can process information in nuanced, rigorous, and healthy ways. So much of the current political discourse is dominated by fundamentalist assertions of truth that seek to villainize rather than understand, to exclude rather than integrate, leading us further down the road to fascism.

On a more basic level, intellectual development allows us to discern what is true, to assess information and assertions. This is especially true today, in an age in which we are drowning in information, much of it false. The inability of our populace to assess what is true and false in the media is a genuine threat to democracy, and a failure of our education system.

Practice, Process, Pedagogy

The activities and processes of the next section will all have an element of inquiry. The teacher is called upon to begin with asking questions rather than giving answers. In this way, the shared wisdom, already present among the students, is drawn out. Whereas a teacher may know more than each student regarding a given subject, the students collectively know more than they are given credit for. And by asking questions, we suggest that, perhaps, the teacher doesn't know everything, and the students are not empty vessels in which to deposit information. Questioning our world is how we learn to think; and how to think, not what to think, is the purpose of the classroom.

The intellectual work here emphasizes wisdom rather than mere knowledge. This isn't that we reject or devalue knowledge; rather, we recognize that wisdom encompasses knowledge:

- Wisdom comes forth from the ability to perceive the whole; knowledge is from a group of isolated facts.

- Wisdom is perceived through the imagination; knowledge is through grasping information intellectually.
- Wisdom is expressed through creativity; knowledge through information.
- Wisdom requires compassion; knowledge is ethically neutral.
- Wisdom and knowledge are not opposites; knowledge is required in order to be wise.

With the sacred circle established, a facilitator cultivates wisdom by first modeling this sense of curiosity, wonder, and epistemic humility.

SOUL: FEELING THE STORY

As an undergraduate at the University of Chicago, I distinctly recall sitting in seminars and becoming aware that I had an emotional response to something we were discussing. I knew, however, that this wasn't a place to share my feelings; this was an *intellectual* institution, a place of higher learning. I suspected that my peers had feelings, too (they were, after all, human beings). I realized that to navigate higher education, one had to suppress one's feelings, or, perhaps, convert those feelings into an intellectual position. I suspected that many of the intellectual positions proffered in class were actually feelings in disguise.

This isn't merely about finding a space for emotions. If there is an emotional response to something that's discussed, rather than bypassing or intellectualizing that feeling, integrate it into the process itself. What is this emotional response teaching us? How can we take care of each other?

This requires the educator to model the healthy expression of emotions. So much of teaching is modeling, and nowhere is this more relevant than in social–emotional learning (SEL). SEL refers to learning and development around interpersonal skills, building self-awareness and -reflection capacities, and the practices that foster deep inner work. Sadly, SEL is still only a part of the curriculum at a small minority of schools. And when it is present, SEL is often only a marginal aspect of the curriculum, separate from the content of the curriculum, and generally considered something that is employed to make young people more successful students rather than being of value for its own sake.

You will note that I have integrated SEL into Chapter 8 as part of what has traditionally been referred to as "social studies." To begin with, social studies must have a liberatory lens. SEL can and should a part of a this broader, liberatory frame. In other words, we cannot expect the student to understand their inner state without recognizing the broader context and issues that affect it.

Meditation, rites of passage, and other healing rituals can offer an approach to this inner work that is rooted in traditional practices and epistemological frames. (These practices are described in greater detail in Chapter 6.) Meditation and the cultivation of mindfulness is an important foundation for emotional health. Rites of passage build community and, as we shall see in Chapter 6, provide a context for group processing. Moreover, rites of passage, as practiced in traditional cultures worldwide, give a young person a sense of place in the world and in community.

All this produces not merely personal growth for achievement and success in school, but a culture of care and community. It is in such environments that learning and growth can flourish. This means that the classroom must be both mindful and compassionate. And it is only when there is a space created for healthy emotional responses to a narrative that a truly rigorous response can occur. This isn't merely about personal healing and peace, but also about collective healing and liberation.

Practice, Process, Pedagogy

This is the time where we engage the subjectivity of the subject matter and of the student. We are not mere thinking beings, detached from our bodies and hearts; nor are we mere physical bodies, containers for chemical reactions. We have an interior life and can cultivate compassion by recognizing the subjectivity of others.

This applies not merely to human beings. The non-human world has subjectivity; groups of people have subjectivity.

As educators, we engage this aspect of human experience first by modeling. The notion that an adult ought not to ever be vulnerable or express emotion teaches the child to conflate maturity with emotional repression. There are obvious healthy boundaries that must be honored, but this doesn't mean we cannot share genuine emotions.

A general emphasis on mindfulness is found throughout this book. And, indeed, mindfulness is among the most important practices and skills we can impart. The way one engages the interiority of self and other in each subject is through mindfulness practice.

HANDS: EMBODYING THE STORY

Among the strangest things about the modern classroom is its failure to properly acknowledge and integrate the body into the pedagogical process. This is the product of a broader pattern in Western civilization of a radical dualism between body and mind and pervades nearly every aspect of society. But it's particularly odd when dealing with youth; for the lives of children and adolescents simply cannot be separated from their bodies.

Think of the five-year-old wiggling in her seat, the preteen's hormonal responses to her environment. Our pedagogies largely consider the body, in examples such as these, to be a problem, a hindrance to the learning process, punished or medicated away. We focus, perhaps, on disruptive behaviors without acknowledging that these behaviors are less mental decisions than they are embodied responses.

We know, for example, that our responses to trauma are largely embodied. So often, our young people struggle in school not because they lack the intellectual capacity or academic skills, but because they are struggling with trauma and stress. And this must be processed not merely through mental exercises, but also through embodied practices. Meditation, mindfulness, yoga, and martial arts are traditional practices that can be employed to help youth work through trauma and foster mindfulness and connection to the world.

The work of philosopher and educator John Dewey is particularly informative here. "Give the pupils something to do, not something to learn," he writes, "and the doing is of such a nature as to demand thinking; learning naturally results" (Boydston 2008, p. 161). Dewey was a philosopher who believed that praxis and ideas informed each other, and he put his ideas into practice in the formation of the University of Chicago Laboratory School. Hands-on activities and embodied practices are not an alternative to mental or intellectual work; they interact and inform one another. Rigorous academics come alive when they are applied in the world and one's hands and bodies are involved. We learn, in a real and tangible way, if those ideas are valid. And sometimes, those ideas can even be modified or rethought.

Practice, Process, Pedagogy

In practice (the reader will find more specific examples in Chapter 6) this can include embodied practices like those mentioned above, as well as project-based work and hands-on practical life work. Project-based work involves engaging with and seeking solutions to the problems and injustices in the world; practical life involves hands-on activities like cooking, building, or managing our daily affairs.

There is no subject that does not involve the body. This, at times, involves a simple awareness of and attention to the body—an aspect of mindfulness. As one engages the interiority of a subject, there is also a physical, embodied aspect.

Moreover, one of the best ways to teach and learn is through hands-on projects, especially when applied through a liberatory lens. One can learn about a scientific concept more deeply through lab work, of course. But the subject matter can be engaged even more deeply if one considers the ways in which science and technology can enhance or harm and works together for ecological justice.

As educators, it is good to pause here and recognize that our work in the classroom is also a form of hands-on learning, the laboratory where theory gets put into practice. This is where our ideas about teaching and learning are tested. Most teachers have learned how to teach only a little bit from theory, but mostly from doing the work. It is important, of course, to reflect and think through how things work in the classroom. But we should not minimize the pedagogical wisdom that comes from this practice. For the people we work with, not just children but also community members, offer a wisdom of lived experience that should be heeded.

OIKOS: EXPANDING THE STORY

Oikos, from which the word ecology is derived, means "home" in Greek. It refers to the sense of place and relationships therein. When we discussed the body, the mind, and the soul, we referred largely to teaching to the individual. This is about the self beyond the individual, the relational self. It is an acknowledgement that no student ever enters the classroom alone; each brings a complex web of relationships and experiences that make up the self.

We can think of ourselves and our world as a mandala, a series of concentric circles. At the center of this self is the soul, our interior lives. Next is the mind and body. From there we move into relationship: the classroom, the community, the society, the world. The language here can vary, but the important thing is that we begin to understand ourselves in relationship, especially to the non-human world.

It is here that a connection to land and place and local bio-region are emphasized. Just as the classroom itself can and should be the natural, ecological world, the activities of the classroom engage with this world, fostering a sense of connection to the more-than-human. Farming and wilderness education expand both classroom and the students' sense of self-in-relationship, fostering a sense of embeddedness and connection to the natural world. Indeed, our loss of this sensibility lies at the root of many of our global crises.

And let us not forget that the global crisis isn't merely one of warming climate; it is also a crisis of meaning and of relationship. An ecological worldview is about relationship, and this can and should include human relationships. So, the activities of the classroom, even when they are not outside or dealing with what we think of as "nature,"[1] can reflect an ecological sensibility through emphasizing relationship, interconnection, and systemic thinking in human relationship.

Practice, Process, Pedagogy

An ecological pedagogy means, first and most obviously, getting outside and engaging with the non-human world. Among the great tragedies of modern life is the alienation of the human from the natural processes of which we are a part. Our alienation from nature and the Earth is not merely an educational issue; it is a problem for our species. We are destroying the planet, in part, because we have managed to delude ourselves into thinking we are separate from it. For any educational program to truly be subversive, it must challenge the dominant paradigm in the industrial world that has estranged us from the Earth.

This also means creating processes that reflect the relational nature of the ecosystem. Human culture is essentially the product of ecological relationships. Our identity as individuals is tertiary. It arises out of, first, our embeddedness in nature and, second, our embeddedness in sociocultural relationships. A classroom is no different. Its processes, therefore, should reflect our ecological, sociocultural, and relational nature.

CREATIVITY: REIMAGINING THE STORY

The work of the student is not merely to perceive the world as it has been given to us; it is to reimagine and transform it. We began the process with community building. This involves sharing our stories—how we came to be who we are and where we came from. *Listening* is essential in this process. It's about our stories as they have been given to us, our selves as they are.

"I Am" poems or other creative sharing processes are a way for youth and elders to get to know one another; to contemplate who they are and how they came to be; to grapple with the complexity, nuance, and paradox of their identities. At a certain point, perhaps at the end of a year or season (depending on the specific structure of the program) we would return to these poems and rewrite them. In this way, we could reflect on how we'd all grown and evolved. For a person isn't merely complex and paradoxical; they are also always changing.

This is a process of reimagining our stories, not merely about ourselves, but about our world. Through the previous processes, we have created a space to reimagine who we are, to reimagine the world. Now, as artists, our youth can express this new vision. For it is through art that the student becomes a teacher. They've reimagined their stories; at Wisdom Projects, through films, books, sculptures, graffiti and more, our students have shared their new vision with the world.

It's important to note that *all* people are artists. Rather than something that occurs in specialized classes or by specialists, art is fundamental to this pedagogical process. We are also limited by what our notions of what art consists of. In most schools, for example, literature is taught through rational analysis and writing as a purely technical skill. And while it is true that intellectual inquiry and technical skill can and should be part of our approach to the arts, it's also true that literature is indeed an art; it also requires an engagement with our feeling, intuitive selves and our creativity. Even less obvious to most is the idea that creativity plays a role in a whole range of human endeavors not typically called art. For example, activism and protest are arts. And sometimes this is the culmination of the learning process for more politically engaged youth. Remember, this is about sharing a vision for transforming our world and part of the role of the activist is to educate.

Art and creativity are not separate from the fundamental creative processes of the universe. We have evolved from single cells through the inherent creativity of life; the dance of predator and prey brings forth the myriad forms that life takes. The lion and the antelope co-create one another, co-create their world. For the human, creativity comes in the form of culture. We transform our world, co-create it, through art, symbol, and story.

There is a liberatory element to this work. The stories of the Bible that were used to oppress and pacify enslaved people came to be seen as stories of liberation, through a new lens. At this moment in human history, the new stories, the stories required for our shared liberation, won't come from the slave master, from the conventional methods of education, or even, perhaps, from our elders. The creativity of the youth is an asset, a vehicle for liberation. Given the right guidance, they can and must be our teachers.

Practice, Process, Pedagogy

The creative aspect of teaching and learning is both beginning and end. The student's engagement with any subject, idea, or skill is not merely technical and intellectual; it is intuitive, creative, and imaginative, and it is rooted in story. The educator's role is not merely to convey information or facts; rather, the educator tells a story, contextualizes information or, more precisely, helps the student gain the skills to integrate information and create their own narratives.

This is where the student's creativity comes in. Every subject is creative, every student—every person—an artist. The response—one could think of this as an alternative to testing—

is the student's creative work, the story they tell about the ideas and skills they learn. In this way, the student becomes a teacher. The recursive learning process comes back around.

THE WHOLE: INTEGRATING THE STORY (REIMAGINING THE WORLD)

The pedagogy began with the formation of the classroom community—rooted in the principles laid out in Chapter 2—and has flowed through processes that incorporate the whole human. The student has not merely become a whole individual; they are now communal, cosmic, and interconnected to the world. In becoming reimaginers of their worldview and teachers of their peers, they are also positioned as liberators. And indeed, the classroom must be a context for liberation. For the purpose of education is not merely to create a better classroom experience, but to bring forth a better world. In this way, the work of the classroom, transformed through these holistic processes, becomes the work of the world.

Practice, Process, Pedagogy

Throughout the educational journey, connections and interconnections are made among various concepts and subjects. After all, there really is only one world, and the cultivation of a singular worldview is what education does—whether one chooses to acknowledge it or not. A curriculum that recognizes this singularity also must recognize that there is only one classroom. The work of the educator, in part, is to help the student find connections. Science and the arts or spirituality are different lenses, perhaps, and use different language, but the integrative work in the end is to reimagine the story that connects those subjects.

The ultimate purpose of education, of course, isn't to create a better classroom, but to create the conditions for the student to bring forth a better world. But classroom and world are essentially the same thing. Integration occurs not merely among the subject matter; it occurs as the microcosm of classroom encounters the macrocosm of the world. This should never be lost on the educator: that the very important work the child performs in the classroom is deeply connected to the work they will do in the world.

NOTE

1. The term "nature" is problematic insofar as it refers to the non-human and excludes the human. *We are nature.* So, in a sense, nothing, even human-constructed spaces, is not nature.

Part II

Reimagining the Class-room

What exactly would such a reimagined approach to schooling and childhood look like in practice? What you'll find here are not comprehensive lesson plans, but examples of activities that can be applied in various learning contexts—homeschooling with the family, traditional classrooms, community centers or churches—and with different age groups.

While I've divided these into "subjects," we ought not get too hung up on rigidly separating them. In fact, one of the benefits of a reimagined school—or a homeschool—is that we don't have to be so particular about the division of subjects, which is more about the mechanistic structure of a school than about the most effective way to learn anyway.

Chapter 4 explores science and math through cosmology and ecology, rooting this study in the vast, overarching story of our becoming and in the web of ecological relations to which we can connect in our own lives. Chapter 5 reimagines the arts through literature, theater, and plastic arts; Chapter 6 focuses on fostering mindfulness and compassion through the cross-cultural study of world religions, meditation, and martial arts practice. Chapter 7 is what Montessori educators call "practical life," learning through hands-on activities. Finally, in Chapter 8, we explore social–emotional justice, integrating a study of justice in the broader world with restorative practices among youth and elders.

***

Whether one is in a homeschooling environment, a school, or any other learning space, it is important to focus on the role of the parent or educator. The lessons and activities in these chapters are not simply a way for us to give the child concise skills or information. Of course, one must be concerned with the development of skills and about learning information. But the primary role of the educator is to create the context for those skills and information. This means that what is most important is the cultivation of a rich learning environment as described in Chapter 2. Moreover, the lessons here are invitations to engage in the material through a holistic process of inquiry and imagination as described in Chapter 3.

Above all else, it is essential to remember that play is fundamental to all learning, at all ages, and in all settings. When young children are engaged in imaginative play, they are learning. While this may be more obvious with young children, it's true for all of us. Older children (and adults) can be playful when they are creating something, when they are engaging in conversation about ideas, and in many other ways.

In other words, these activities represent only a beginning—an invitation, if you will—a way for adults and children to begin the process of exploring and reimagining their world together.

Chapter 4

Cosmos

Science and Math through Cosmology and Ecology

Among the most popular trends in education today is an emphasis on STEM (Science, Technology, Engineering, and Math). While the renewed emphasis on hands-on learning that comes with technology and engineering has its benefits, there is an unspoken reduction of math and science to that which is most beneficial to the global capitalist system. Certainly, technology can be employed to, say, reduce pollution or benefit the global south; but, if we are honest, this is seldom emphasized. Moreover, an overemphasis on that which is marketable—whether it is a job or a product—stymies the cultivation of a deeper understanding of scientific principles, a contextualization of the scientific principles in the bigger picture, and a sense of awe and wonder. From a holistic standpoint, the foundation of science should not be in rigid compartmentalization, abstraction, or technical jargon. Rather, it should rest on the foundation of the following:

1. *Cosmology: the big picture.*

   Cosmology is the story of the Universe and how we fit meaningfully into it. According to modern science, we have evolved from a singularity and everything and everyone is connected, part of the same evolutionary process. Whether we are studying chemistry, physics, or biology, the overarching cosmology provides the context and meaning for all of modern science.

2. *Ecology: the evolution of life and embeddedness in the natural world.*

   Just as it is important to understand the big picture, science also asks us to explore our specific, local place. Ecology is the foundation of the way life functions on earth and of the interconnection of all life.

3. *Advocacy: finding meaning and purpose from science to help the world.*

   Our approach to science cannot be divorced from ethics and social issues and, therefore, address issues like ecological justice, climate change, and the ethics of technology.

4. *Awe, wonder, and curiosity.*

   Finally, our children (and adults) should find awe, curiosity, and wonder in the world. This, not the fixation on jargon or abstraction, will bring us the next generation of scientists.

What follows are examples of concepts and practices that I have implemented through my work with the Chicago Wisdom Project, Wisdom Projects, Inc., and in my own home. They can be adapted to various age groups and contexts. Moreover, they can serve as a springboard to create and co-create—with your children—new activities.

COMMUNITY

We begin with the notion that the classroom and cosmos—or school and world—cannot entirely be separated. Our community, therefore, isn't merely a group of people with whom we are studying or learning, but the layers of concentric circles extending throughout the cosmos. The world, in other words, is our classroom.

In this way, the classroom is a context for the cultivation of planetary consciousness, a space in which to instill a sense of connection to the whole. The individual isn't merely a part of a local community, but also a member of a global one. The study of science requires this sense of grandeur and awe, of a community that extends beyond that which the human has made. And at the same time, the classroom of the cosmos can be rooted in the local bioregion and in ecological principles. The small is as much a part of the cosmic community as the vast. But while cosmos and *oikos* are about the natural order of things, the classroom must also reflect the inherent wildness of wilderness.

In practical terms, we begin to cultivate this community through the establishment of the sacred circle, the learning space. One way to think about this is that to conceive of the world as a cosmic circle, we can create a literal circle in the classroom. This means establishing a culture and process that establishes the learning process itself as sacred and linked to the larger processes of the Universe and the natural world.

When at all possible, this is an opportunity to acknowledge the world as the classroom. A garden can be a classroom; a forest can be a classroom. A starry night can be a classroom. Too often, our classroom is shrunken down, offering merely a diminished version of the human and the world. If nothing else, science is a study of the world, creation, the cosmos, and it should yield awe and wonder—everything else comes forth from that.

INTELLECT

If there is a fundamental intellectual error in the way our schools approach science, it is the lack of context. The general approach is to focus on methods and concepts as foundational, rather than on narrative and context. For example, by the time a child reaches the age where they begin a more serious study of science, they will be introduced to a series of abstractions, coming in the form of either (a) lab work that primarily serves the purposes of teaching scientific methods rather than instilling in a child a sense of wonder and place in the world or (b) concepts that, while foundational to the study of science as an academic field, are relatively meaningless for a child.

Instead, the focus of scientific study must begin with the narrative. Before we get into the cosmology based on the scientific narrative (which I will refer to as "the Universe story") we should understand more about what a cosmology is and some alternative cosmologies. This begins with an inquiry into the nature of myth and narrative.

A cosmology always comes in the form of a story. This is true of science as well as myth. There are, of course, epistemological differences between scientific and mythic approaches to the world, but the aim of neither is to merely convey knowledge—it is to integrate knowledge into a coherent story. The scientific approach has the advantage of a rigorous method that is open to change; the mythic approach has the advantage of being conscious of the values it conveys.

So, rather than beginning the study of science with scientific methods or abstraction, we begin with an exploration into the nature of cosmology and narrative. This is entirely rooted in neuroscientific understanding of how the brain works, and we should be teaching based on this brain science. For we understand now that we process information through story. This is why, for example, giving people more facts about climate change doesn't affect their belief about it.

The story of scientific cosmology, therefore, begins with the creation myths that preceded it. This can come in forms students are familiar with, such as the Bible. But it can and should also include creation stories from various cultural traditions. None of this is about teaching religion; rather, it is an investigation into the nature of human consciousness.

For modern science, this means the story of the Universe—the broader story within which all studies of science (and history) fit. It is the way to understand physics, astronomy, geology, chemistry, biology, and anthropology. There are many ways to tell this story, but here is an example:

> *The story of the Universe is the story of each of us. Each phase, each moment in this story is the Universe giving birth to us. Each moment represents the birth of our common ancestor.*
>
> *Out of unimaginable light the Universe was dreamed into being. It contained all the light, energy, and potential for everything that would ever come to be, all contained within the vessel of hydrogen.*
>
> 1. *The Primordial Fireball (13.7 billion years ago).*
> 2. *Stars (13.3 billion years ago).*

3. *Galaxies (12.7 billion years ago).*
4. *Expansion (7 billion years ago).* Dark energy overpowers the gravitational pull of dark matter and the expansion of the universe accelerates.
5. *Supernova (4.6 billion years ago).* Our mother star, in the Orion arm of the Milky Way galaxy, having consumed and sacrificed herself, collapsed. In the intense energy of that collapse, she was transformed into a supernova, exploding her stardust into space, and birthing all the new elements which would take shape as Earth's body and ours.
6. *Sun (4.5 billion years ago).* That exploding stardust began to slow down, cool, and condense into a community of planets around the mother star, our Sun.
7. *Earth (4.1 billion years ago).* Our planet slowly cooled and gradually formed an atmosphere, oceans, and land mass.
8. *Life (4 billion years ago).* Gradually, within the oceans, more complex arrangements began to take shape. These were the first simple cells, and through them, Earth awakened into life.
9. *Photosynthesis (3.9 billion years ago).* Earth learned to take nourishment from the Sun. Through these simple-celled microbes, she learned to eat sunlight, to nurse from the Sun. And that dynamic laid the pattern for all future life forms, that each must receive nourishment from another, and give itself in return to become nourishment for another.

10. *Sexual reproduction (1 billion years ago).* Life was mysteriously drawn toward union, and the first simple-celled organisms began to reproduce sexually. Different strands of genetic memory were combined in the new offspring. This opened infinite new possibilities. Around the same time, organisms began to feed on other organisms, and that relationship formed the basis of the community in which each would develop.
11. *Birds (150 million years ago).* The first birds took flight, and in and through them Earth broke into melody and song.
12. *Flowers (120 million years ago).* The first flowering plants emerged, concentrating their life energy and memory into seed, making protein in the form of seed available for the mammals who were yet to come, and, in their flowering, bringing color and fragrance to Earth.
13. *Mammals (114 million years ago).* The first placental mammals developed, warm-blooded creatures who, like the supernova, carry their unborn young within their own bodies, and who nourish them from their own substance both before and after their birth.
14. *Earliest hominids (2.6 million years ago).* The earliest hominid types evolved from the primate mammals in Africa. Creatures with brains and nervous systems complex enough that in and through them Earth awakened into self-conscious awareness of her existence.

15. *"Eve" (70,000 years ago)*. Our common ancestor, our great-grandmother, "mitochondrial Eve" lived in Africa. There were only 2,000 human beings at this time. Soon after, some of these humans began to leave Africa to populate the rest of the Earth.

Science, when contextualized this way, is a story of our becoming. Each subject is an emergence of an ancestor:

- *Physics* and *astronomy* are stories of our past—when we look to the stars, we are seeing our ancestors, all the way to the birth of the Universe. (Numbers 1 through 6 above)
- *Chemistry* emerges with the chemicals created in stars, the foundational elements for life on earth. (Numbers 5 through 8)
- *Geology* is the study of the Earth, which emerges in the context of the formation of the solar system. (Number 7)
- Life is not merely static; it is understood primarily through evolutionary processes. Indeed, even if one studies the workings of the human body, this is best conceptualized as part of a bigger story of evolutionary emerges. This is *biology*. (Numbers 8 through 13)
- Human cultures emerge in the context of the biological emergence of the human. This is the foundation of *anthropology*. This isn't to reduce human culture to biology; rather, it is to understand humanity in its broader, cosmic context. (Numbers 14 and 15)

It should also be understood that conceptual mathematics can be a part of the story of the Universe, too, particularly as it pertains to physics. Moreover, even for small children who won't be able to study physics, numeracy and conceptual mathematics is just as important as the practical. I've often heard it said that math must be rooted in practical matters—budgets, taxes, and so forth—and this is true (more of that in "practical life"), but equally important is a deeper understanding of the context for math in the cosmos and the underlying concepts at the root of numbers.

SOUL

There is a danger—and perhaps this is a fundamental error of Western civilization—in radically separating one's inner life from the outer. I earlier referred to the "inner climate"—the interior world that cannot be separated from the outer world, and as such, its crisis is yet another a context for, and not separate from, the climate crisis. Our inner work—whether it is meditation, therapy, or shared rituals—always have a cosmic context. (We will explore this further in Chapter 6.)

Too often, science neglects the very aspect that makes one want to explore science in the first place, the cultivation of awe and wonder. And this can only happen if we are immersed in the world. Moreover, it requires an attitude of openness and joy and inquiry. A part of all scientific exploration must involve this sense of intimacy, joy, wonder, and, especially, curiosity about our world.

Just as one's inner life—the sense of relationship to and care for the natural world—can fuel the inquiry in which scientific exploration depends, the immersion in and engagement with nature can also feed the soul. Too often, our inner work is alienated from nature. But to educate in a holistic way, one must recognize the inner life is integrated with the embodied, intimate with the ecological and cosmological webs of relationships.

A paradox of the scientist is that nearly everyone who becomes a scientist does so because of a curiosity and wonder about the natural world. This somehow tends to get lost in the classroom. In our classroom, an intimacy with nature and mindfulness practices that maintain this connection to, and love of our world remain central to scientific study. After all, the purpose of cosmology is to identify one's place in the cosmos, to find relationship, not merely detached objectivity.

In this way, the Universe story is not merely a way to understand a process that is separate from us; it is the story of us, the story of our ancestors. Each moment is the birth of an ancestor and, as such, a rite of passage, a moment when one type of being in the world passes away and another is brought forth. It is not unlike the passage from womb to world or the way that a young person, by learning together in community and growing in mind, body and soul, becomes a new kind of person with a new role in the community.

HANDS

The study of science and mathematics must be both conceptual and practical, abstract and tactile. The hands-on aspect of the process is where learners who need to touch and feel to understand are most comfortable. For many children, mathematics is best understood through tactile techniques.

The Cosmic Walk

The cosmic walk is an exercise to understand the story of the Universe according to modern science. A 140-foot rope can be used to represent the timeline of the Universe. Numbers should be marked to scale on the rope to indicate each new emergence in the story of the Universe. The rope can be made into a large spiral. Each student chooses a particular number or, if the group is smaller, students can walk along the rope as the story of the Universe is told.

The value of this exercise is not only found in the scientific knowledge acquired; rather, it is an opportunity to ask big questions about our place in the cosmos and to reflect on our interrelatedness. Moreover, it offers an overarching narrative—a big-picture context—for all further scientific exploration. Begin with some questions:

- Where do we come from?
- What is a creation story?
- What purpose does it serve?
- What are some examples?

One thing I love about this activity is that it can be used with any age group. Of course, the older and more advanced the group, the more detailed and complex the conversation can become. But it's also an embodied engagement with the subject matter. When I used it while homeschooling my own children (who were ages five and seven at the time) we would race across the yard as the exploding, expanding Universe.

There are many discussion points from this exercise. How do the students feel about the scientific account of the Universe? Is it overwhelming? Does it feel meaningless? Do they prefer it to the religious accounts they may have heard? The task of the facilitator is not to tell the students what to believe; rather, the teacher should ask the students to accept the story for now and consider what it might mean for how we treat one another. What if each moment in this story represented the story of our own becoming? What if this were the story of our ancestors and us? What if we were all related? How does this story relate to other creation myths? Finally, have the students make a timeline of their own lives—past, present, and future—marking the points of emergence (rites of passage) in their own lives.

To this point, the focus has been largely on engagement within the classroom and within the human psyche. But hands-on learning is also a time to move beyond the boundaries of the classroom and into the world at large. Science, ecology, and cosmology are above all an engagement with the natural world. While it is often true that the conventional classroom places limits on this engagement, we can also find ways, through camps and nature retreats, to cultivate a sense of relationship to the other-than-human world. Wisdom Projects retreats were designed by participants in collaboration with a facilitator, so they varied from season to season, but they generally included the following:

1. **Check-in, Ritual Beginning of Retreat. This should be similar to the ritual opening of all sacred circle activities: everyone comes into a circle for a meditative practice and check-in.**
    - Personal check-in with each participant in the circle. Each person can share what they are feeling (physically or emotionally) as much as they feel comfortable.
    - The responsibility of the other students is to listen without interrupting.
    - The facilitator can interject but should also model listening.
    - Return to seasonal themes and questions or the theme of the retreat.

2. **Nature Activities**
    - Silent walk: a meditative walk through the woods
    - Star walk: people in urban settings seldom see the stars at night. This can be one of the most powerful experiences at a retreat.
    - Plant/bird identification: This can include common, indigenous, and scientific names, as well as medical and traditional uses.

3. **Quiet Time for Reflection/Journaling**
    - An important element of any retreat is quiet time for reflection. This can include meditative practices as well as solitary nature activities.
    - Each participant has a journal, to be kept at the retreat center.

4. **Fire Pit**
    - Every evening, participants gather at the fire pit to socialize as a group and to reflect.
    - At times, a formal ritual may be part of the fire pit experience. For example, this can be a context for an opening, closing, or rite of passage ritual.
    - Other times, this may simply be a time to share stories or music.

5. **Significant Free Time**
    - As much as anything else, the retreat is a time for youth to bond as a group. The retreat facilitators should allow for youth to self-organize and to relax together. There is a tendency among educators or youth workers to over plan and try to manage the time of the youth. A major context for learning is the way that youth self-organize and determine their own use of time.

6. **Practical Life. A retreat can be an opportunity to live together in community, sharing tasks and responsibilities.**
   - Youth should take responsibility for a variety of roles at the retreat.
   - Preparing food is especially important, as mealtimes are a time to gather as a group. Moreover, learning to prepare food with ingredients from our gardens can become part of healthier lifestyles.

7. **Ritual and Rites of Passage**
   - In one example: Youth in our programs have generally split up into boys' and girls' groups. But it is important to be aware of an find a space for nonbinary students. The facilitator is responsible for setting the tone and creating the sacred space. A talking stick is passed around. Everyone in the circle is to understand that only the facilitator and the person with the stick should speak, and no one should speak out of turn (even if their comments are meant to be helpful). The responsibility of everyone in the circle is to remain present for others. Going around the circle once, each person shares his greatest joy; going around the circle again, each person shares his greatest fear; the last time around, each person shares his greatest pain. At the conclusion, the circle can be opened for discussion, but the talking stick should still be used. The sacred circle should be ritually closed at the conclusion.

8. **Sharing of Creative Work**
   - The retreat can be a time for youth to share what they've done both at the retreat and throughout the year or season (see Chapter 4).

9. **Ritual Closing/Reflections/Gratitude**
    - It is important to close the circle, too, and to offer a time for reflection and gratitude.

***

Another hands-on way to explore science and cosmology is through farming and food. Food can be grown, prepared, and eaten together. Businesses can be created with the produce.

So many of us have no connection to or awareness of the source of our food. But even if we don't grow our own food, an awareness of its source can be cultivated from a young age, and myriad connections and lessons can be made from this. At any age, we can bring or make food and challenge the students to come up with a list of factors that were required for it to be there in front of us. For example, if the snack is a piece of fruit, the list might include:

- Sunlight
- People who picked the fruit
- Soil
- Oil for transportation
- Rain

The list could obviously become quite long as the students begin to consider the web of relationships that allow us to obtain our food. The instructor should provide an example. Using a large piece of paper, have the students make a simple diagram with their food at the center and lines connecting it to the items on the list. Then have the students draw lines connected all the places where they used the same source. Identify what is necessary on the list (e.g. healthy soil, water, etc.) and what is unnecessary and external that are damaging to the natural process (non-local or -seasonal products, oil/petroleum). This exercise is a way to (1) cultivate an awareness about the seasonal cycles from which we are often so detached and (2) expand our sense of who we are and our interconnections to a vast, living world.

Lastly, science and math can and should be employed for the purposes of *advocacy*. Young people can be hands-on not merely because this is an easier and better way to learn; our youth can also learn by engaging with science as it affects their communities and their world. This begins by teaching through a social justice lens. With groups of teens, we've introduced the concept of "environmental racism" as a way for youth to understand how ecological destruction is not merely an issue that concerns the privileged, but something that, in fact, impacts the poor more than the wealthy, Black more than white, global south more than global north.

OIKOS

Ecology and evolution are central in the study of life and of the natural world. Ecology is the way that life exists in relationship; evolution is the way that life transforms and grows in relationship. Any understanding of our natural world must be grounded in these central facts.

The human is fundamentally placed in this ecological and evolutionary web. Consider the story of hawk and mouse:

> *Mouse spent his days running from Hawk. Hawk was so fast, his vision so precise, that Mouse could sometimes barely get enough food for his family. Hawk required him to be constantly vigilant. The friends and family members who were Hawk's victims required Mouse to create stories of remembrance. He was tired in body and in spirit.*

> *So, Mouse prayed to the Great Mouse in the Sky. "Please, oh Great Mouse, please grant me this wish. I pray that you would make Hawk a little slower so that I could feed my family more easily and suffer less."*
>
> *The Great Mouse in the Sky granted this wish. For a time, life was easier for Mouse. But soon he began to slow down. Soon, Hawk was giving him problems again. So, he returned to the Great Mouse in the Sky and again asked for Hawk to slow down. And again, the wish was granted.*
>
> *For a time, things were easier. But again, in time, Mouse slowed down. He returned to the Great Mouse and again asked for the same thing and again it was granted.*
>
> *This repeated itself until Hawk could no longer fly and mouse could barely run. Mouse had no more stories to tell.*
>
> *Mouse was no longer Mouse.*
>
> *One last time, he returned to the Great Mouse in the Sky and asked for one final wish to be granted: "Please, oh Great Mouse. Please make Hawk faster."* (Richards 2018)

The point of the story is that hawk and mouse co-create one another. The shape of our legs, our teeth, our minds do not come from some extrinsic power; they were created by the speed of the lion and the gazelle, the grains we ate, the weather patterns of the African plain. Our bodies and the stories we told were created—like this book—through natural, relational processes. So too must the shape of the classroom, the curriculum, and our pedagogy.

When we understand our place in ecosystem and cosmos, the study of ecology and cosmology turns into a study of the self. The role of the parent and educator is to teach our children that they are at once not the center of the world and, at the same time, the center of the universe. They are immeasurably small and unimaginably vast. This is the central lesson of cosmology and ecology.

CREATIVITY

Recently, there has been some acknowledgement, by inserting the "A" in the rebranded concept of "S.T.E.A.M" (Science, Technology, Engineering, *Arts*, and Math), that creativity can and should be a part of science education. This largely comes into play in the design aspect of engineering, for example. And indeed, it is important for our youth to engage in the creative process of building and design. But there are other, less commonly applied ways to integrate creativity and imagination into science education.

While the tactile and practical dimension of mathematics are important, math is also an exercise in the abstraction requiring the imagination. A child must be able to use the mind to conceptualize numbers and their relationships. In this way, math does not merely serve a purpose; it trains the mind to work in a particular way—through abstract, imaginal thought. To be sure, this isn't the only way to think and learn, but it is still important.

Ecology is partly a way to understand the inherent creativity of life. An ecosystem is a web of relationships, of course. What's more, it is a web of relationships creating and recreating life, imagining and reimagining life. Life evolves through the intrinsic creativity of this web. This is the foundation of human creativity and of the creative energy of the classroom. We do not learn as isolated individual on our own individual paths; rather, we learn in relationship. Content does not merely exist in some concrete fashion; it emerges through the intrinsic creativity of the classroom.

By grounding the study of science and math in cosmology, we recognize that the human cannot be separated from natural processes; there is no objective study of nature. Rather, we study nature as a part of nature, as an expression of nature, as nature. The mandala can serve as a visual conceptualization of this concept. Using a template of concentric circles, our students have drawn or painted their own mandalas—symbolic maps of the cosmos and themselves. The mandala places the individual at the center; each subsequent concentric circle a more expansive aspect of the self.

We might also return to the "I Am" poem with science in mind. At times, we have used more specific prompts to reflect more specific subject matter:

> I am [something you have created]
> I am [something you envision creating in the future]
> I am the story of . . .
> I am [someone or something in your ancestry]
> I am [a rite of passage experience in your life]
> I am [a rite of passage experience in the story of the Universe]
> I am [something in your ecosystem/bioregion]
> I am [an issue of environmental (in)justice]
> I am [a kind of tree]

In general, it is important to understand that the cosmos itself is an expression of the intrinsic creativity of the Universe; a cosmology is how human beings, through human culture, express their understanding of the order and beauty of the Universe and their place in it. While perhaps there is an objective cosmos out there, our understanding of it requires human creativity to bring it forth in a meaningful way.

INTEGRATION

All the subjects addressed here are inherently fluid and interdisciplinary, and the study of science, cosmology, and ecology are no different. Let's look at how this subject can be integrated with the others.

Arts: The cosmos is an expression of the creativity of the Universe; a cosmology is the story we tell about it. The arts are fundamental in integrating the ideas of science into a coherent and meaningful worldview.

Spirit: Our schools—rooted in the Modern worldview that would radically separate spirit and matter, science and spirituality—tend to think of science and spirituality as oppositional. But the myths of our religion serve the same fundamental cultural purpose as a scientific cosmology. In addition, cultivating connection, mindfulness, awe, and wonder are part of one's spiritual life and scientific endeavor.

Hands: Science must be rooted in the hands-on work of not merely the lab, but the world. Building, growing food, and exploring nature and wilderness are fundamental aspects of science.

Justice and Joy: Science and technology do not necessarily have to be considered ethically neutral. In addition to the application of nature through mindfulness practice and hands-on projects, we can apply and study science in order to work toward a more just, sustainable, and compassionate world.

The purpose of the study of science, cosmology, and ecology is to create a more robust sense of the whole, to cultivate in each a sense of our interrelatedness and connection to the whole. This classroom is seeking to develop a world-vision that allows for human civilization to live harmoniously with

Earth. We cannot lose sight of the centrality and urgency of the ecological crisis and how educating differently is essential in addressing it. Creating a different kind of classroom—an ecological classroom—brings forth a different world-vision and a different kind of civilization, an ecological civilization.

Chapter 5

Arts

Literature, Performing Arts, Visual Arts

Taking an integrated approach to school, the arts shouldn't be relegated to something that only happens in art class. It's central to the way we all learn and should be a part of any subject. Just as the concept of "cosmology" above provides a philosophical and scientific framework for knowing our place in the world, the arts offer an opportunity for people to discover and express their place in the world through story and symbol.

It is also noteworthy that literature is included in the arts. Too often, schools take an overly technical approach to teaching reading and writing. As with any art, there is of course a technical aspect to writing, but there is an equally important creative side.

While literature often tells a story in a straightforward way, all arts is fundamentally an act of mythmaking, world-making, through story. The word "poet," at its root, means "maker." And, indeed, the poet and the artist are makers of the world through story, a process known as *mythopoesis*.

COMMUNITY

This subject is fundamentally about this sharing, and any genuine community is one in which stories are shared. Before the reimagining of the story can even occur, it is important to establish the classroom as a space in which to listen and to be heard. Each member of the learning community brings a story, each member already an artist. Often, a young person already has a deficit narrative. This is okay; the work of the teacher isn't to change the narrative; rather, it is to create a space for the youth to change the narrative themselves.

It is the sharing, the space in between the individuals, where the art happens, where the meaning is brought forth. Rather than thinking of a work of art as having a concrete meaning, let's think of it as pregnant with meaning, and that cannot entirely be said to exist until it encounters another. This is not unlike—metaphorically if not literally—the concept in quantum physics in which the exact location only exists when it is observed. We bring forth meaning in art through observation, too, or, more precisely, through the relationships of a community.

The learning community is a context for creative expression and play. In focusing on play rather than competition, the emphasis is shifted from product to process. The classroom is a community of people lifting each other up and giving space for play and creativity. The concept of constructive criticism and feedback are tied up in notions of community. That is, if we take seriously the notion that a classroom is a community, we can support each other as we wrestle with the creative process. Good art requires this kind of support, this kind of space—the space in which we can experiment and play rather than focus on a finished, marketable product.

In putting together an actual, physical learning space, we can think of the space itself as art, rather than a place to put art. Let's consider the kinds of things that are often put on the walls of a typical classroom: posters trying to inspire kindergarteners to get into college or excel on standardized tests or explaining the virtues of the semicolon. None of these things will impact the young person in any way other than to rob them of their agency. One of my favorite classes in high school was "Cartooning and Graffiti" with Mr. Berry. In part, Mr. Berry was an effective teacher because he never told us what to create—that was always our choice. But I also recall the wall of his classroom, where students would bomb graffiti. But it doesn't have to be art as such that the students put on the walls, or even involve the walls. Consider that it is the work of the learning community to create the learning space. When we do this, we can think of our *lives* as art. As the poet and potter M.C. Richards puts it, "The big art is our life." (Richards 2011, p. 41)

INTELLECT

All arts are an intersection of technique and creativity, mind and heart. While we tend to think of imagination as something that stands in opposition to intellect, it is more useful to think of them as part of the same creative process.

Unlike other arts, literature is often approached from a strictly technical and intellectual angle. Students learn grammar and various forms of literary analysis; even poetry is reduced to one's ability to identify various forms and techniques. Often, students are graded on rubrics regarding their ability to identify various literary techniques—what could be less poetic than that! What's missing, of course, is the intuitive, emotional, imaginative aspect of literature. There will be more on that below, but it's also worth looking at what a genuine intellectual approach to the arts would entail.

Let's begin with asking some questions—an inquiry, if you will, into the symbols of culture. Our youth are more inundated with information than ever before. They are drowning in it, in fact. Participation in the democratic process, in the culture as a whole, requires us to be able to recognize the narratives we are given. This requires a rigorous analysis of the arts and media. What is the story they are telling? What are they trying to sell? What are they trying to make me feel in order to buy what they are selling? By asking questions like these, we can analyze the ways in which our cultural narrative influences consciousness.

Social media has come to dominate how we engage in the arts, and it is important to analyze not merely the arts, but the medium itself. When it's appropriate (and this age seems to get lower every year) it can be useful for students to keep a "plugged-in" journal. Sometimes—this is true for someone of any age with a smart phone—we just don't realize how much time we are spending in front of a screen. And this is an opportunity to really study the media we use and how it affects the brain. Moreover, it affects whom we communicate with, how, and what information we see. This is an essential element of anyone's education in today's world.

Let's also return to the notion of technique and the arts. So much emphasis is placed on that which is testable and quantifiable. For example, just as we overemphasize literary techniques when we analyze literature and poetry, we also overemphasize things like grammar in teaching writing. It's not that grammar isn't important; it's that the way we teach it often reduces good writing to its technical elements. One learns to write, in general, by reading good literature. And, of course, by living one's life deeply and meaningfully. This is how we come to find our voice as an artist.

Technique is best discovered not by testing or rubrics, but through a mindful process of balancing the beautiful and the technical, and by mentoring and apprenticeship. It is worth considering, as well, the role of mentorship and apprenticeship in education. We assume that to be an educator means to be a teacher—and that a teacher must be an individual authority figure standing over a group of students. But a teacher can also be a mentor, a student can also be an apprentice. These kinds of one-on-one relationships can be important for the young artist.

SOUL

I again draw from the work of Matthew Fox. In his graduate programs in spirituality, Fox implemented a holistic pedagogy in which, in addition to the more intellectual aspects of the course, there was time for embodied practice, emotional processing, and what he called "Art as Meditation." It was during this period that students were encouraged to engage in practices that involved various artistic practices from drumming and dance to pottery and poetry. For Fox, this was a way to engage the ideas with the right brain as well as the left. (McSweeney 2020) Moreover, it was a reimagining of the whole notion of meditation—and art. For the purpose of Art-as-Meditation is never the product; it is always the process, and the subtle changes we go through when we are creating something. "Only art as meditation reminds people so that they will never forget that the most beautiful thing a potter produces is . . . the potter," he writes. (Fox 1983) And while there is, of course, a place for silent meditation, there are also more active forms of mindfulness practice, such as embodied practices (see "hands" below) and the mindfulness of engaging in creativity.

At Wisdom Projects, we have often used theater and especially improv as a way to explore our emotions through the arts. For example, "Sound Ball" is a way for participants to tune in to one another in a creative, embodied way:

1. Have the group stand in a circle.
2. One person makes a sound—any sound—while also making a throwing gesture toward another person in the group. That second person then "receives" the sound with a physical motion like catching a ball or a sack or a ray of light and—importantly—repeats the sound sent to them.
3. Then, without hesitation, the first receiver sends a new sound with a new gesture to another person in the circle.
4. Keep the sound moving quickly and boldly to get everyone involved.
5. Make sure to get the body involved and not just the voice. An active, athletic stance—like you would need if you were prepared to catch a real ball—helps loosen up the mind.
6. Encourage participants not to predict or plan what sound they'll make if the ball comes their way. Better to receive the one sent and then send a new one that emerges of its own accord. Make sure that participants do actively receive the sound sent to them before sending one out. It's a great affirmation to the sender and helps build a spirit of generosity.
7. Add in your own variations as your group gets better with Sound Ball. We've played City Ball, Vegetable Ball, Names that Start with M Ball, and so on. Keep encouraging folks not to have one waiting in the wings to use. Or, even better, let them have a response in the wings—but then choose another one in the moment.

Theater in general, and especially improv, also offers a way to learn to express one's emotions creatively and safely. The actor doesn't merely "pretend" to feel a certain way; they draw from their own experiences and feelings and, in this way, can safely and creatively express and process them.

HANDS

The arts are *embodied*. Some examples are obvious—dancers and actors literally turn their bodies into art—but all arts are embodied. The movement of the painter's brush, the flow of the singer's or poet's breath—these, too, are embodied.

At Wisdom Projects, we've used the potter's wheel to engage in the meditative practice described by M.C. Richards as "centering." The potter's wheel, moving in a circle, requires the artist to center the clay, focusing with precision on the single point of awareness at the center of the rotating circle. This activity is done with both mind and hands. One's hands feel the wet, textured clay as the circle spins, centering and focusing the mind to create a work of art. This requires a deep listening. Richards writes:

> And with listening, too, it seems to me, it is not the ear that hears, it is not the physical organ that performs the act of inner receptivity. It is the total person who hears. Sometimes the skin seems to be the best listener, as it prickles and thrills, say to a sound or a silence; or the fantasy, the imagination: how it bursts into inner pictures as it listens and then responds by pressing its language, its forms, into the listening clay. To be open to what we hear, to be open in what we say. (Richards 2011, p. 9)

As with poetry and literature, plastic arts also require one to learn technique along with creativity. With the potter's wheel, hands and heart and mind come together to produce a reimagined product and a reimagined self.

OIKOS

At its core, the arts are a specifically human expression of the inherent creativity of the evolving cosmos. Human creativity isn't separate from the Earth's creativity; art becomes a part of our evolving cosmos.

The classroom can connect to the Earth's creativity reflecting the embeddedness of the artist. Below are some examples of ways that creative activities can reflect this embeddedness.

Mandalas of Suffering, Pain, Struggle

Students describe an episode of suffering, pain, or struggle in their lives and community. For example, we once worked with a group of high school dropouts, many of whom had been incarcerated. They had been told, repeatedly, that their "poor choices"—strictly as individuals, had led to their situation.

The participants then recreate the mandala of concentric circles. From this mandala, what they create shows how that episode is related to each circle—their family, their community, and their world (this can vary a bit). They begin to see, through this process, that everything in our lives is connected, and that we have some agency and responsibility, of course, but there are other factors, beyond our individual control.

Indeed, this is a truer understanding of *karma*. Literally meaning action, *karma* refers, in Buddhist and Hindu traditions, to how the world is created, co-created, and recreated through our actions and thoughts. But this never happens individually. We are always embedded in relationships.

Next, the students create a mandala of support, showing how their peers, their family and their community can support them through their struggles.

Multi-Perspectival Roles Activity

In this exercise, the students explore the different roles they play. Students make a list of the roles they play in their family, at school, and in their community (or "the street"). To understand the notion of roles, the facilitator can demonstrate her or his roles in each case. Students learn to express the different roles they play by describing three roles in a particular context, one that is a noun (for example, one might say "a brother"); one that is a verb ("nurture"); and one that is an adjective ("funny").

Students share the lists. What do the lists say about the importance of context? Depending on this context, how do our roles change? Do the roles we play sometimes seem to contradict each other?

Finally, more advanced students might reflect on the following paradox:

a. There is a "Self" that transcends these roles; we are more than the ways in which others define us.
b. Our "Self" is not isolated from others; in many ways, "who we are" is defined by our relationships.
c. [For advanced students] The "Self" is empty—that is, there is no fundamental self or ego at our core; we are deeply interconnected and made up of a web of interconnected relationships.

CREATIVITY

What, after all, is creativity? As described above, the arts require technique, mindfulness, and imagination. And creativity is how we put the imagination into action. Creativity dances on the edge of chaos and cosmos, disorder and beauty. Good art cannot be too rational, too orderly, but it transforms the chaos into beauty and order—*cosmos*. Matthew Fox explains:

> What do we do with chaos? Creativity has an answer. We are told by those who have studied the processes of nature that creativity happens at the border between chaos and order. Chaos is a prelude to creativity. We need to learn, as every artist needs to learn, to live with chaos and indeed to dance with it as we listen to it and attempt some ordering. Artists wrestle with chaos, take it apart, deconstruct and reconstruct from it. Accept the challenge to convert chaos into some kind of order, respecting the timing of it all, not pushing beyond what is possible—combining holy patience with holy impatience—that is the role of the artist. It is each of our roles as we launch the twenty-first century because we are all called to be artists in our own way. We were all artists as children. We need to study the chaos around us in order to turn it into something beautiful. Something sustainable. Something that remains. (Fox 2004, p. 7)

As educators, we must learn to navigate the chaos of childhood, some of which is rich and pregnant with creative potential. But we must also recognize that there is trauma in the chaos of childhood. And even if this pain contains a seed of creative potential, we cannot gloss over the trauma and should strive to implement trauma-informed practices.[1]

As always, we begin with some questions. What does chaos mean? Why should we study chaos? How has chaos come up in my own life? What happens when people are afraid of chaos, try to crush chaos by controlling everything? An important point is that *chaos is not simply disorder. Chaos explores the transitions between order and disorder, which often occur in surprising ways.* Note the moments of chaos in the learning process and, similarly, note the moments when things become excessively ordered. What is a good balance for you? How is this balance being met or not being met? Below are some examples of ways we have approached chaos with students to better understand how beauty and creativity can arise out of the chaos.

Chaos in History: The Middle Passage is an example we've used of a group of people whose lives were thrown into chaos. This was not a mere tragedy. For those who endured the Middle Passage, an entire world and worldview was eradicated. In its wake, in a new world, they came together to become a new people, with a new language, a new culture, new stories. Indeed, from the chaos of the Middle Passage, a culture arose that would influence and transform the entire world. There are also specific examples of historical figures who dealt with chaos and transformed it into something positive.

Chaos in Mythology: What do our religious traditions say about chaos? There is a pattern found in many creation myths of the cosmos—our ordered world—arising out of the primordial chaos. The words chaos and cosmos come specifically from the Greek mythological tradition. In many other traditions, there is also a tradition of the Trickster. The Trickster's role is to challenge boundaries and norms—to play with the edge of cultures and worldviews, doing things that might be considered inappropriate or even evil. But the Trickster's role is to force us to grow and change by confronting our own absurdity. In this way, the Trickster is the primordial artist, the challenger of what we think is possible.

Chaos and Science: Chaos theory helps us to understand that science isn't always predictable. Chaos in the evolutionary process demonstrates how growth and transformation occur not merely despite chaos—they require chaos.

Chaos and the Arts: We have already looked at the Middle Passage and slavery as an example of chaos in history. What were some of the creative forms that emerged from this experience? Jazz, blues . . . others? Hip Hop emerged in the 1970s in the South Bronx, an area that had been devastated by drugs and violence.

How have any of these examples changed your ideas about chaos? Which of the above examples are a metaphor for the role you play in the world? Think of chaos as letting go of our need to control or attachment to a specific outcome. How will this affect the creative process?

Above all else, perhaps, creativity is an invitation to explore one's unique gifts.

1. Remember a time before you had responsibilities like homework. How did you choose to fill your days?
2. Think of a time when you lost track of time. What were you doing?
3. What is something you are good at? This may or may not be in school.
4. What excites you?
5. What makes you feel alive?

Lastly, let us return to the "I Am" poem, with a particular emphasis on that which we can create out of chaos.

> I am [an example of suffering I have experienced]
> I am [an example of suffering in the world]
> I am [an example of chaos in my life]
> I am [an example of chaos in the world]
> I am [an example of order or creativity that arises out of chaos]
> I am [an example of a warrior]
> I am [an example of something that arises out of silence]
> I am [an example of something that arises out of darkness]

INTEGRATION

The world is intrinsically creative, co-created by the webs of ecological relationships. The work of the artist is to express, in a particularly human way, the inherent creativity of the world. Rather than a discrete subject, it makes more sense to think of the arts as the expressive element of any subject.

> **Cosmos**: While the study of science is largely about observation and analysis, there is also an oft-neglected creative aspect. Because we are emphasizing cosmology, the next, and essential, step is the creation of a narrative around the observation and information. The scientist and the artist are partners in the process of creating this narrative; or, what's more, we are all scientists and artists.
>
> **Spirit**: The role of the artist is not unlike that of the shaman or mystic. Or even the Trickster. Just as organized religions evolve when people challenge accepted beliefs,

cultures and civilizations are transformed by the artist. Moreover, the work of the artist is inherently spiritual in that it is rooted in the interior life, the soul of the artist.

Hands: Whether it is cooking, parenting, or gardening, our daily work is art.

Justice and Joy: The work of creating a more just world is creative. It requires not merely to become angry and seek change, but also to imagine the possibilities. Moreover, the work of healthy political engagement is an *art*. The symbols and rituals of activists are art. This is not just a way to challenge power, or even to bring more people to a cause; it also is a way to experience genuine joy and community in the solidarity of movement-building.

Ultimately, the role of the artist in any society will determine a great deal about the kind of civilization we create. Fascist or totalitarian regimes always come for the artists. For it is the artist who sees things from different perspectives and with nuance. The civilization that listens to its poets, embracing paradox and nuance, moves away from fascism.

NOTE

1. See Chapter 6.

Chapter 6

Spirit

Spirituality, Mindfulness, Meditation

Education isn't merely about skills and information. Fully realized, education can and should consider bigger questions about our place in the world; promote kindness and compassion; and offer practices to help calm the mind and look within. Just as cosmology is the big picture—the way that everything is a unique expression of and connected to the whole—spirituality is the interiority of things, the notion that there is a subjectivity and inner life of each being.

In this chapter, we approach this aspect of life, but some clarification is in order. Rather than thinking of spirit in opposition to matter, or spirituality as radically separate from nature, let's think of the spiritual as:

- **The interiority of things**: It isn't that the spiritual stands in opposition to the material; rather, it is another dimension of the whole. It is the interiority, the feeling, the intuitive, the sensual.

- **An opportunity to ask Big Questions**: We all have a desire to consider the whys of our life. This shouldn't merely be the purview of the privileged.
- **That which seeks connection**: There is a useful place for making distinctions and creating categories. Indeed, this is one of the primary ways in which modern science has both been effective and contributed, to a certain extent, to a worldview that envisions us as radically separate from one another and the natural world. The spiritual—philosophically and in practice—is the work of seeking connections.
- **A vision of the whole and our place in it:** By nature, spiritual cosmologies always present a vision of the whole. As such, they are never precisely accurate in the way that a scientific vision is. They emphasize sense- and meaning-making over precision. This is neither better nor worse, but a useful and different lens.

COMMUNITY

What makes up a community? There are, of course, many ways to answer this question depending on the particulars of a given community. But it's important to ask not because of those particulars (i.e., describing who is in the community) but because how we answer teaches us about how we think of community. For "community" is an overused word. We talk of "online communities," for example, that are mere networks of people with shared interests. For the sake of this subject, I argue that a learning community—and, indeed, any community—requires three-dimensionality, depth, and attention to the inner life of each member.

In this way, a learning community must be a context for one's inner life, a space in which to share, process, and heal. So, just as an individual has an interior life, a soul, so, too, does a community. This is the aspect of depth in a classroom, the way in which learning space should be envisioned not merely as a flat surface in which to interact, but as a space in which each individual and interaction possesses a rich interior life.

The educator is not separate from this process. Genuine humility requires a recognition that we are not only learning together; we are growing together. The teacher, as well as the student, is asking difficult questions about their world, seeking healing from trauma, and working toward a more mindful and meaningful life.

INTELLECT

Religion and spirituality have been a neglected aspect of education. In parochial schools, of course, there is education specific to a particular faith, but often this amounts to little more than indoctrination. At best, it is limited to a specific tradition. Public schools often shy away from dealing with religion, or at least approach it from a merely sociological perspective. On the one hand, there is a fear of alienating more religious families; on the other there is the belief among the more rationalistic that religion offers nothing of value.

But religion is a fundamental aspect of the human experience. If nothing else, to understand something about our religious traditions is to understand something deep and true about what it means to be human. Moreover, religion, like another other form of human culture, has healthy and toxic forms; or, better put, it has mature and immature forms. Many of us engage religion at about a kindergarten level, which explains why it is often rejected or expressed in a simplistic or toxic way. So, rather than thinking of a religion as either good or bad, we can think of ways of approaching it that would be helpful for the intellectual and spiritual development of the student. Not all Christians, for example, are fundamentalists who would damn all non-believers to hell.

Following are some ways we could explore various religious traditions.

Myth: All religious traditions begin with a story: the Buddha's journey from opulence to awakening; the exodus from slavery to freedom; Muhammad's struggle to unify and convert the Arab world; the creation stories from every culture and people on the planet. Too often, we begin with information or, worse still, lists of rules. The story doesn't merely reflect the emergence of the tradition, it also places the individual in relationship to that tradition. For better for worse, it is the ultimate expression of the values of a culture.

Ritual: Rituals are extremely important for young people. It is how, in a tactile and practical way, they begin to learn their place in the world and to know what to expect. Rituals and ceremonies from the world's religions add another dimension to a child's routines and practices; for an authentic ritual gives one a sense of place in the world through embodied and communal activities.

Seasonal cycles: Rituals are generally connected to seasonal patterns and cycles. Obviously, these vary depending on one's location, but global patterns, such as solstices and equinoxes, are found in most spiritual traditions and are celebrated through seasonal rituals. In this way, the cosmic aspect of a tradition becomes more explicit, and we can learn how different traditions are rooted in the same universal patterns.

Ethics: While surely it is true that one doesn't require religion to be ethical, many traditions offer a lens with which to approach deep and important questions about what makes a good life and how we ought to treat one another. At its best, a religious tradition asks questions rather than dictates rules, but nonetheless helps us to grapple with how to live a good and ethical life.

Mindfulness: Mindfulness refers to the way we cultivate awareness and presence in our bodies and in the present moment. We'll discuss ways that we can approach mindfulness in the classroom below, but before doing so, it is useful to understand the cultural and spiritual tradition that such practices are rooted in.

Cultural context: While it is useful, to be sure, to explore the universal aspects of spiritual traditions, it is also important to better understand their cultural context, an endeavor that serves to foster a broader cultural literacy and respect for diversity.

All these can form the intellectual foundation for deeper work, collectively and individually. "All men [sic] are intellectuals," writes the Marxist philosopher Antonio Gramsci, "but not all men have in society the function of intellectuals." (Gramsci 1971, p. 9) Gramsci is pointing out that there are classist (as an Italian Marxist, this was his primary lens) and racist biases that underpin the way we think of intellectual work and philosophy. We all want—and, indeed, *need*—to consider big and difficult questions about our lives and our world. But often the work of genuine philosophical inquiry is considered somehow inappropriate or unnecessary for marginalized groups. The emphasis, we are told repeatedly, should be on vocational training. And in doing so—even among the well-meaning—their marginalization is exacerbated. This is no argument against job training—the next chapter will address that—but it is an argument that holistic education invites us all to become philosophers. This benefits the world as a whole; for new insights can come from those who may see the world differently from those in power. But it also benefits the individual; for a life that is examined and a world that is questioned is a more spiritually healthy one.

SOUL

The soul work of the classroom is both collective and individual. First, through rituals and rites of passage, the community comes together in shared, transformative experiences. For the educator, it is important to understand that rites of passage and seasonal rituals are important developmental and community markers for a child.

A rite of passage is a ceremony, ritual, or set of activities that marks the transition from one phase of life to another. It may also refer to the process of change an individual goes through while moving from one stage or role in life to another. Birth, the passage from womb to world, is the prototypical rite of passage. It is an initiation into this world, and from one kind of being in the world to another.

Initiation is about the creation, maintenance, and continuity of the community; it is how cultural knowledge and wisdom is passed on to successive generations: When a person is initiated, it means they are now responsible to pass on wisdom to the younger generation. What is the wisdom you hope to pass on to younger youth? To your children? Roles are defined and redefined: What are some examples of roles in a community? What role do you see yourself growing into in the future? For example, your current role may be as a student, but one day you might be a teacher. It's about finding our home, knowing who we are and where we come from and belonging to a community. When someone asks who you are, what do you say? An initiation helps us to understand this question in a particular way. For example, we might understand that we are a part of a people whose roots stretch back thousands of years. The experience of our elders and ancestors is a part of who we are. As part of this self-definition process, we realize that those who came before us are a part of us.

Traditionally, an initiation is when one is made a member of a sect or society. Initiation is about learning, being tested, and taking on new responsibilities. Examples include coming of age ceremonies, confirmations, bar or bat mitzvahs, or quinceañeras. It can also involve partnering—when things come together, such as an engagement, marriage, or a business partnership—and endings, a time of finishing or letting go, such as death, retirement, or graduation.

A "coming of age" ritual is the most common form of intentional initiation. The community helps young people transition from child into adolescence; traditionally the intent is to shift the focus of youth toward their roles in the community. This form of rites of passage is particularly relevant in the classroom. How can we integrate and welcome students into the sacred circle in ways that are culturally relevant, sensitive, and unique? How can we honor the achievements and transitions of students?

As with rites of passage, meditation and mindfulness can be applied to the modern classroom in a way that honors the traditions from which it came, but also does not require a strict adherence to those traditions.

Mindfulness refers to a form of consciousness in which we are awake and aware of our world, our minds, and our bodies. The Buddhist meditation teacher Thích Nhất Hanh explains:

> People usually consider walking on water or in thin air a miracle. But I think the real miracle is not to walk either on water or in thin air, but to walk on earth. Every day we are engaged in a miracle which we don't even recognize: a blue sky, white clouds, green leaves, the black, curious eyes of a child—our own two eyes. All is a miracle. (Nhất Hanh 1999).

Meditation is a practice that helps to sharpen this awareness. Its benefits are well documented: it can cultivate resilience to stress, enhance compassion, improve mental health, positively impact relationships, and improve physical health. (Smith et al. 2017) But we ought to be careful about thinking of meditation only as a means to an end. This kind of utilitarian thinking—that we can appropriate traditions in order to become better workers or students—misses the entire point: that we are deeply interconnected and fundamentally members of a community rather than individuals.

When working with younger people, taking an approach that involves a variety of methods and seeing what works is most effective. Here are some suggested practices:

Outside mindfulness activities: Walking meditation is good for anyone, especially young people. It allows for one to practice mindfulness while moving. Encourage them to notice their surroundings—what did you hear, feel, see?—while being fully present in their bodies.

Use an altar or props (incense, stones, statues): Altars or special meditation rooms send the message to a child that this is a different kind of space. Sometimes, special props can help a child engage as well. Sometimes we hold a small stone while in meditation. This is also an opportunity for young people to learn about different contemplative traditions.

Emotions: After sitting silently, we take the time to explore and name our emotions. This is a way to build emotional awareness and intelligence. Other times, we may focus on one kind of emotion. For example, we might ask what we are grateful for. Or, as Cleis Abeni teaches, we might find a word that makes us feel happy and peacefully repeat it, first at loud, then quieter and quieter until it is in our breath.

Martial Arts: If you have this kind of training, martial arts can be an excellent way to interest young people in meditation. For example, some traditions talk about imagining the body as a tree, rooted into the earth, its branches reaching up into the heavens. Simply imagining oneself as a tree is a great practice for children. Another, slightly more sophisticated notion is yin and yang—seeking to find the balance externally and internally between the hard and the soft elements of ourselves.

Lastly, it is always good to encourage people to simply sit with their breath. For small children, encourage them to lie on their backs with a stuffed animal on their belly and observe the animal rise and fall with their breath.

***

In any learning environment, educators must implement trauma-informed practices. This means that a teacher must understand how trauma impacts the classroom collectively and individually and implement practices that seek to heal rather than punish. Trauma isn't merely about a painful event and its memory; trauma can change bodies and minds, mentally and chemically, and induce responses that can be difficult to comprehend if we are not educated. Physician and addiction expert Gabor Maté explains:

> The greatest damage done by neglect, trauma or emotional loss is not the immediate pain they inflict but the long-term distortions they induce in the way a developing child will continue to interpret the world and her situation in it. All too often these ill-conditioned implicit beliefs become self-fulfilling prophecies in our lives. We create meanings from our unconscious interpretation of early events, and then we forge our present experiences from the meaning we've created. Unwittingly, we write the story of our future from narratives based on the past . . . Mindful awareness can bring into consciousness those hidden, past-based perspectives so that they no longer frame our worldview . . . In present awareness we are liberated from the past. (Maté 2011, p. 370)

The traumatized child may react to a situation because they are flooded with chemical and hormonal reactions in the body. While their reaction may seem irrational in the moment, one must understand that these responses are often a matter of survival. This cannot be punished away. Genuine healing often requires more than what the teacher can provide in a classroom setting, but the healing process can be enhanced by trauma-informed approaches and by the fostering of genuine community and care.

HANDS

It has been clear throughout that a healthy, holistic approach to education requires a rejection of the dualism between spirit and matter, body and soul. Trauma is partly an embodied response, whether or not the initial trauma was physical. Healing practices, therefore, all contain an embodied aspect.

Martial arts, for example, are a physical practice that also contains a healing element and deeper, spiritual elements. To begin this journey, we can consider the distinction between a "warrior" and a "soldier." The idea is that, as our children enter into adulthood, they will become warriors.

- Both warriors and soldiers must show courage to fight: What are some things that are worth fighting for?
- A warrior fights peacefully; a soldier only fights violently. Discuss different types of "fighting"—for example, the term "*jihad,*" which can refer to both an inner and outer struggle.
- Peaceful fighting: fighting for a cause peacefully or nonviolently, like sit-ins/die-ins or protests. What is a way that one can "fight" without using violence?
- A warrior only uses violence when all other possibilities have been exhausted; a soldier fights because he is told to fight: How does one discern when to fight and when to walk away?
- A warrior thinks for himself; a soldier follows orders: What is an example of a time not to follow the orders of authority?
- A warrior fights external battles (for justice) and internal ones (in the soul); a soldier can only fight others: What is an internal battle that you struggle with?
- Who are the warriors in our communities? In the world today? Who are the soldiers in our communities? In the world today?
- We can discuss and process an example of a conflict in the classroom. As the conflict is described, one group acts out the issue from the perspective of a soldier, the other as a warrior.

The Chinese martial art of *bagua zhang*, rooted in Taoist and Confucian cosmologies and philosophies, offers an example of a martial art that, while it does teach fighting and self-defense, also contains healing and spiritual practices that benefit the whole person. In the practice, the following are some of the principles learned.

Circles: All movements in bagua are circular, just as the cosmos itself is circular. In combat, power is generated through coiling circular movements and escape from another's grasp can happen through circles. This mirrors the learning principle of circles in which the classroom, and world, are circles.

Yielding: When seeking to escape or evade, the practitioner learns to yield rather than use brute force. This teaches us that there is power in softness.

Wu Wei: Often translated as "active non-action," *wu wei* refers to a way of dealing with conflict that seeks harmony with one's opponent and with our world. This does not mean we passively accept things as they are, but that we can and should learn to make change through harmony rather than violence.

***Yin* and *yang*:** The Taoist/Confucian worldview describes a cosmology in which there is a balance between the soft and the hard, the light and dark, the passive and the aggressive. These forces exist on a macrocosmic level and, in the human, as a microcosm. The practice in conflict is to find this balance. Healing comes from finding this balance within.

All of these concepts can be put into practice in the study of bagua, not by learning the philosophy but by engaging in hand-on practices. It is important to note that these practices, like yoga or other embodied spiritual practices, require skilled and trained instructors—they cannot be learned from reading a book. These traditions are passed down from teacher to student. My martial arts teacher, Sifu Tony Roberts, always used to tell us that he wanted us to not just be good martial artists, but also good teachers. He mostly taught silently, allowing the students to teach each other. The first day a new student entered the classroom, they were asked to teach something, anything, because Tony believed we are all teachers, and all have something to learn. In traditional arts like bagua, the relationship between teacher and student—influenced by the Confucian emphasis on relationship—is foremost. The teachings are passed on from teacher to student—and the students then become teachers.

ECOLOGY

Eco-spirituality and deep ecology are ways of understanding and experiencing our ecological place in the world. The Indian activist and philosopher Vandana Shiva (2016) has critiqued the Western worldview and its impact on the environment as rooted in patriarchal notions of control and epistemology. Indigenous agricultural practices, often held by women, have been rejected in favor of more extractive, utilitarian, and, ultimately, harmful practices rooted in industrial capitalism. She equates the capitalistic domination of nature with the patriarchal domination of women.

Deep Ecology is a philosophical tradition, first posited by the Norwegian philosopher Arne Næss (2010), that ecology isn't merely about understanding ecosystems from the outside, but also about recognizing the human as fundamentally ecological. Human consciousness, therefore, is as much a part of the ecosystem as plants or animals. Deep Ecology is about engaging that consciousness in a way that, rather than something external that observes, it is the ecosystem's way of observing itself.

Eco-spirituality is the practice of fostering this consciousness. Mindfulness practices in nature, for example, can help cultivate this consciousness while fostering a love for and connection to the wild. We used to begin all Wisdom Projects' retreats with a "Silent Walk," wherein students would simply walk through the woods together. Later, they might reflect on how their senses were awakened during the process. A similar activity required the students to silently seek out Easter eggs with questions or quotes inside. The idea was to work together and to move mindfully, pay attention, and find all the eggs. The group would discuss the ideas in the eggs afterwards.

Any community and any classroom can ground itself in seasonal rituals and earth-based rituals that connect us not merely to the interior life, but also to find a deeper connection to the world around us. At Wisdom Projects, we have designed curricula based on the four seasons. And many of the traditional rituals and spiritual practices are rooted in the seasonal, lunar, or solar patterns. Moreover, growing and preparing food can bring us closer together and closer to the earth and its patterns. Ritualizing these practices places a deeper emphasis on our connection to them.

CREATIVITY

Whereas traditional religions have often simply given practices and stories to people, the spiritual work of the student is to reimagine rituals and stories. Let's think of a classroom as a place where, at this crucial moment in human history, we can creatively reimagine those traditional rituals and stories.

INTEGRATION

One approach to the interdisciplinary aspect of this subject is to recognize that each field also has an interiority.

Cosmos: As the universe evolves in complexity, it also evolves to possess a deeper subjectivity. The inner life—consciousness, the soul—isn't separate from the world, but it is the world knowing and feeling itself. Moreover, when we tell a story of the world, even one that is informed by the scientific process, we are engaged in deep spiritual work.

Arts: The work of the artist is fundamentally spiritual work in that it engages with the intuitive, interior consciousness.

Hands: Our spiritual practices all contain an embodied element. This includes both shared rituals and individual practices like yoga and martial arts.

Justice and Joy: Spirituality involves both an ethical component—how we engage the world beyond us as individuals—as well as a way to find joy without looking away from the world's suffering.

In the end, the purpose of a spiritual practice, like a classroom, is to foster a particular kind of world-vision. Here, I would like to emphasize the importance of a healthy interior life and the primacy of relationship. Our worldview often neglects these aspects of human experience—or at least relegates them to the margins. A healthy spirituality recognizes that one's interior life and mental health are of the utmost importance. Moreover, it shifts the emphasis from individual to relationship.

Chapter 7

Hands

Practical Life, Work, and Hands-on Learning

If a classroom is a microcosm and a space in which to prepare a child for the world they will create and inhabit, then it also is a space to prepare them for the work they will do. A child's work, as much as an adult's, is profoundly important. It can give them a sense of purpose and meaning, of ownership and agency. Moreover, children co-create their world through work. A child's work doesn't only occur in the learning space; it can also be the way that the child co-creates the classroom.

I've borrowed the term "practical life" from the Montessori model. This simply means that one learns not just from information or theory, but also from a variety of practices that are woven into daily life. Such activities can include cleaning, cooking, gardening, vermiculture, composting, repairing, or assembling.

There is a hands-on aspect to any learning endeavor. A math problem can come alive when applied to real life experiences or tactile learning approaches; a science project can bring abstract concepts to life. We can even engage the body and movement to instill a deeper connection to an abstract concept or idea.

The importance of the child making their own choices should not be underestimated. "The child looks for his independence first," writes Maria Montessori, "not because he does not desire to be dependent on the adult. But because he has in himself some fire, some urge, to do certain things and not other things." (Montessori 1948, p. 9) We should also not underestimate the child: children can often do far more—and far more independently—than we give them credit for. And even if they do not sweep the floor as thoroughly as we would like, the long-term learning benefits surely outweigh the unswept crumbs.

In this chapter, you will find less theory. Instead, you'll learn about various practices we've employed to educate through work and projects, involve the body in the learning process, and experience the joy and learning that happens when we get our hands dirty.

COMMUNITY

For many years, Wisdom Projects ran retreats for groups of teens. Generally, around 12 students and 6 adults attended. While there were a great number of activities that comprised these retreats, perhaps the most important thing was that which wasn't in the curriculum. Students were responsible for taking care of each other in community. They prepared food and cleaned up, organized schedules and planned activities, carried supplies and created guidelines and boundaries for each other. For a community isn't merely a group of people with shared interest; a community must grapple with how to live together.

Any classroom can become a context for this kind of shared community-building. But this requires the educator to shift their way of thinking about what a classroom is. The educator must have the humility to allow the students to participate in the creation of the space, to engage in their playfulness and creativity to make the classroom, to build it, at least metaphorically, through their work. The biggest impediment to this kind of work is the notion that a classroom's primary function is to provide a space to acquire testable skills and knowledge. With this attitude, having a student clean up, or feed a pet, or prepare food would be considered a waste of time. Time, in the capitalist system, is money—and the industrial classroom mirrors that. But if the primary purpose of the classroom is to create community— as the foundation of all learning—then shared work is essential.

INTELLECT

Hands-on education begins with tactile mathematics for small children. Using money, a rekenrek (counting rack) or an abacus is central to learning numeracy in small children. "The hand is the instrument of intelligence," writes Maria Montessori, "The child needs to manipulate objects and to gain experience by touching and handling." (Montessori 2012)

There are other ways to engage the logical mind through hand-on projects. Organization, planning, and measurement are woven into project-based learning. A classroom ought not be entirely organized by the teacher; rather, it can and should be a context for the youth to organize themselves and the space. This contributes not only to the student's sense of agency and confidence; it also allows the child to think through intellectual questions about how to structure and organize their classroom world, questions that will continually be asked as their world expands.

Let's return, for a moment, to our mandalas. The classroom lies at the center of the mandala. As the scale widens, youth can begin to look at bigger, real-world problems. Just as our youth can answer questions about how to manage our classroom and navigate its conflicts and problems, so too can they begin to address the questions and challenges of the broader world. It is here that we ask questions, solve problems, and engage in our communities and world.

SOUL

Something changes in us when we are engaged in a hands-on activity. Our focus shifts from the busy, overstimulated "monkey mind" to the singular focus of the task at hand. This is true when one enters a Montessori classroom, even among very small children. "At some given moment it happens that the child becomes deeply interested in a piece of work; we see it in the expression on his face, his intense concentration, the devotion to the exercise." (Montessori 1912, p. 346) Indeed, work can be viewed as a kind of meditation or mindfulness practice. Thích Nhất Hanh writes:

> If while washing dishes, we think only of the cup of tea that awaits us, thus hurrying to get the dishes out of the way as if they were a nuisance, then we are not "washing the dishes to wash the dishes." What's more, we are not alive during the time we are washing the dishes. In fact we are completely incapable of realizing the miracle of life while standing at the sink. If we can't wash the dishes, the chances are we

> won't be able to drink our tea either. While drinking the cup of tea, we will only be thinking of other things, barely aware of the cup in our hands. Thus we are sucked away into the future—and we are incapable of actually living one minute of life. (Nhất Hahn 1999, pp. 4–5)

This speaks to the idea that spirituality and mindfulness are embodied. What's more, the purpose of mindfulness isn't merely to be at peace while we are sitting alone in meditation, just as the purpose of the classroom isn't merely to produce academic scholarship or success. Our purpose is to go out in the world with this sense of mindfulness.

We must also remember the embodied aspect of trauma and our healing from it. Working with our hands, in community and in solitude, is a way to be present in the moment, to observe our thoughts rather than fixate on them. And this is an essential aspect of healing.

HANDS

In the end, living itself is education and life is a classroom. Let's consider some of the practical arts that can be integrated into the classroom. Each of the following have been a feature of Wisdom Projects' programming, especially on retreats.

Cooking and food preparation: Young people love to cook. And there are so many lessons in preparing food. Above all, it is a shared, communal experience that enhances relationships and builds community. But it is also a way to learn practical lessons about how to cook. In addition, students can create the businesses to sell healthy food to their peers and community.

Cleaning: Small children love to help clean. While some of the lessons of this caretaking are obvious things like organization and planning, the care of the classroom, like everything else in the learning space, is a metaphor for how one cares for one another and for the world.

Building and repair: The classroom isn't merely a context for a child's work. The classroom itself is the child's work. Youth can make and repair a classroom. An aspect of a nature retreat can be for the youth to put together tents or build a yurt. This, of course, teaches the lessons of measurement and planning. But it also teaches a child that the world is theirs to make and mold.

Let's also reimagine physical education. Gym class and physical education are largely focused on competitive sports. At many of our universities, the football coach is the highest paid employee, in spite of the well-documented abuse of players by coaches, Schools often prioritize sports over things like the arts. I do not wish to condemn or remove sports, but I do believe that it is more helpful and healthy to think of athletics as part of a broader curriculum of health, wellness, and physical fitness.

Physical education should also be a part of a broader wellness program. Along with an epidemic of mental health challenges among our children, there is also an obesity epidemic. Young people have become increasingly sedentary, diets increasingly unhealthy. It's important to acknowledge that there is also a justice aspect to food. This cannot be reduced to mere "choices"—there are economic and historical reasons that some communities have less access to healthy food—but it is also important to educate children about healthy eating.

Lastly, it is essential that sex education be taught from a holistic perspective. This means not merely teaching the science, but also giving young people the space to process their feelings and navigate relationships. Above all, youth must learn to have a healthy and positive feeling about their bodies, free of shame.

OIKOS

The lessons of ecology are perhaps best learned in relationship to the ecosystem. Here are some examples of hands-on practices that can enhance that connection and provide holistic learning opportunities. What's essential for students in all these practices is fostering a consciousness of their participation in the circle of life.

Farming and gardening: At Wisdom Projects, we have run community gardens and food forests. Students learn how to grow food sustainably and, as with cooking, create a business to sell food to the community.

Vermiculture and composting: If we are to share food in community in the classroom and grow food, composting is a way to complete the circle. It shows the children how our waste can return to the earth to be used to grow food. If space is limited, vermiculture (worms) are a great way to turn food waste into soil.

Nature education and retreats: The nature retreats described above are a way for youth to become immersed in wilderness and to participate in myriad hands-on activities. We've learned about identifying plants and animals on retreats; learned how to make a fire and set up a tent; cooked and cleaned and planned. But there is also a subtle—or perhaps not so subtle—shift in consciousness that can occur in a person when they are immersed in nature. Nature immersion is about relating to the wilderness and our own wildness, experiencing ourselves as a part of the ecosystem.

CREATIVITY

Everything described in this chapter involves the child's creative process. Just as I have suggested that the arts ought not be reduced to product, they also ought not be thought of as exclusively the domain of the professional artist. The traditional artisan, for example, is just as creative in their process as the professional painter. The child can be just as creative when they are cooking or sewing or building something as they are in art class.

INTEGRATION

The child who makes something isn't merely making a thing; *they are making a world.* The child who creates things with their hands becomes a creator of culture rather than a mere consumer, someone who can make for themselves rather than shop. A classroom in which children are responsible for caring for one another and the space brings forth a world that is cared for by the people. All this is rooted in the notion that our world is co-created.

Each discipline contains a hands-on, embodied aspect:

Cosmos: This is where we get outside and participate in wilderness activities; engage in science experiments; and apply science in the world.

Arts: As described in Chapter 5, the arts are embodied. They are ideas and imagination, of course, but they are also extensions of and interrelated to our human touch, our breath, our physical bodies.

Spirit: The spiritual aspect of work is found in the mindfulness of being present, in our bodies, and in the moment while we engage in daily work.

Justice and Joy: Part of our work is also about how we create a world. Understood through a liberatory lens, we see our work as creating a more just and sustainable world, whether it is in the form of a paid job or taking to the streets in protest.

A deeper exploration of the meaning of work is needed. And this can perhaps begin with making a distinction between work and a job. So much energy is devoted in our school systems to "job readiness." This speaks to our worldview in which one's value in the world is conflated with their job title or position. Rather than focus on how a child might get a job, the existence of which we cannot know by the time they enter the job market, it is better to focus on the meaning and importance of work. The conflation of work and wage labor in the capitalist system has often served to marginalize or render invisible traditional work and the work of women. With this in mind, work is how we participate in and contribute to our community; find our purpose and meaning; and make, with our minds and hands, our world.

Chapter 8

Justice and Joy

Social–Emotional Justice Studies

To begin, all history or current events are understood through a particular lens. We advocate for a social justice lens—that is, telling the story of history or current events from perspectives other than those in power. What's more, we employ this lens with a *liberatory* pedagogy, a process whereby we do not merely learn *about* issues of social justice, but also seek practices that empower and liberate the student. This is an element often neglected, even in so-called social justice curricula: to observe history or current events through a social justice lens is just a start; how we engage the material—and one another—makes for a liberatory pedagogy.

I have added the "emotional" element because social–emotional learning—the way we treat one another and deal with conflict with the school or home—is the way to teach broader lessons of society. Liberation occurs not merely in learning about issues; it occurs when we simultaneously embrace inner and outer freedom and power. So, we learn about social justice not simply by discussing the pressing issues of today or of history, or even by directly engaging with such issues and seeking to change the world. We must ground those issues in creating more just interactions and relationship within the learning space. Again, the classroom is a microcosm. A just and liberatory learning space brings forth a more just and compassionate world.

Lastly, while our children can and should look honestly at the injustices in our world, this ought not to lead to despair. The pursuit of justice ought to be a joyful endeavor, a practice of both genuine sorrow and of genuine celebration and community.

COMMUNITY

So, we begin with the formation of community as a context for liberation and as a way to support one another in our shared struggle. I would like to contrast the American, capitalist, individualistic notion of "freedom" with the deeper, collective notion of liberation. The concept of freedom in many contemporary circles has to do with one's legal rights as an individual, often contrasted with collective responsibilities. For example, debates about mask mandates or government regulation to protect against pollution are often opposed in the name of "freedom." It is a freedom rooted in a cosmology of loneliness.

Our classroom is shaped like a circle. It honors the unique perspectives of each, values no one above anyone else. This circle is the antidote to loneliness because it allows us to find joy amid the suffering. This doesn't mean that we bypass the pain. We share the pain in community. This is genuine joy, as opposed to happiness or contentment.

The community is rooted in the shared stories about the struggles and injustices in one's community. We aren't yet at the solution stage. This is more about recognizing that the experiences on the ground in a community are valuable and need to be heard. It is important for adults to honor the wisdom and perspective of the youth and particularly important for educators who are outsiders in the community to honor the wisdom that comes from the lived experiences of community members.

INTELLECT

Just as cosmology rests on the foundation of the universe story, the intellectual foundation of social studies is the big story of humanity. And this is on the same timeline. Humanity emerges in Africa through evolutionary processes.

Understanding the thread of this single story is a beginning. It is how we see ourselves, humanity, in a broader context, and see humanity's *singularity*. There is no such thing, biologically, as race. Race is a social construct, invented for the purposes of rationalizing the global slave trade. For older students, approaches such as Critical Race Theory rest on this rigorous understanding of race.

But recognizing the diverse peoples and perspectives is also an important aspect of a liberatory pedagogy. Employing a liberatory lens in our approach to history and current events means that we see the story of history and politics not as neutral, but as an opportunity to seek out a more just and compassionate world. The central questions we must return to, again and again, are: What is the story being told? Who is telling it? Why are they telling it and what does it say about power?

Our intellectual engagement with social justice must also contain an epistemological element. It is often in the how a story is told, and by whom, that we can best analyze it. Because of the proliferation of the Internet and social media, it is useful to begin with media awareness. Youth, if they are old enough to use social media, can consider how much time they are plugged in. Keeping track of this for a week is a good practice. They then must consider the kind of media they are consuming and, as with history, who is telling the story and why.

At Wisdom Projects, we've watched commercials together to analyze images and the narratives various companies offer. What are they telling us about ourselves to get us to buy what they are selling? These questions can also be asked about historical or current events.

SOUL

The soul-work of a liberatory pedagogy recognizes the social and political context for our emotional lives. Mental health is inextricably linked to our world. To reduce it to an isolated interiority is not only inaccurate; it is oppressive to those who deal with collective and generational traumas.

This oppressive attitude about mental health reached its nadir with the rise of "zero-tolerance" policies, particularly prominent in charter schools found in black and brown communities. Bill Ayers and Bernadine Dohrn write:

> Schools everywhere—public, private, urban, suburban, rural, and parochial—are turning into fortresses where electronic searches, locked doors, armed police, surveillance cameras, patrolled cafeterias, and weighty rule books define the landscape. (Ayers and Dohrn 2000)

There has always been a racist and classist assumption in such policies, often unspoken, that certain kinds of children require more rigid discipline than others. This is rooted in the deeply entrenched beliefs about the need to control children generally, and black children specifically. The zero-tolerance classroom is the classroom as prison; what we need is the classroom of *play*.

With this in mind, one approach to shared interior work are restorative practices. Rooted in indigenous traditions of community justice, restorative practices emphasize the restoration of community relationships over punishment. This is because they are rooted in the belief that we are fundamentally members of a community rather than individuals. Robert Yazzie writes:

> Navajo justice is a sophisticated system of egalitarian relationships, where group solidarity takes the place of force and coercion. In it, humans are not in ranks or status classifications from top to bottom. Instead, all humans are equals and make decisions as a group . . . There is no precise term for "guilty" in the Navajo language. The word "guilt" implies a moral fault that commands retribution. It is a nonsense word in Navajo law due to the focus on healing, integration with the group, and the end goal of nourishing ongoing relationships with the immediate and extended family, relatives, neighbors, and community. (Yazzie 1994)

A community is essentially a web of relationships. Trust, responsibility, and compassion are required for those relationships to be maintained. When harm is done in a community, there is a severance of these bonds. Punishment does not restore these bonds, nor does labeling someone as good or bad. This does not mean that people do not do harm or should not take responsibility for harm that is done.

Rather, it means that the emphasis is placed on restoring trust and repairing the relationship.

Like mindfulness and other buzzwords, restorative justice can be implemented in ways that appropriate elements of the practice without truly being a part of a restorative classroom. Restorative justice advocate and professor of education Kathy Evans explains:

> [I]n our haste to implement RJ in schools, we don't lose our way. Not all programs that call themselves restorative are indeed restorative. Many are restorative-ish; others have been completely co-opted so that restorative terminology is used to rename the detrimental programs they are meant to replace. For example, having kids wash the cafeteria tables in lieu of suspension may be a better option, but it isn't necessarily restorative . . . Implementing restorative justice to address behavior without critically reflecting on how curriculum content or pedagogy perpetuates aggression is limiting. (Evans 2014)

Moreover, we must be careful not to forget the indigenous cultures from which restorative practices come. This is a matter of learning respect for the wisdom that has been accrued for generations by these cultures. But it also is about truly embracing the worldviews upon which they are based. Without this, restorative work can be merely another practice to perpetuate an oppressive system.

HANDS

There can be no justice without engaging the world and working for change. This is where the liberatory classroom truly extends beyond the walls. But a word of caution is in order. Too often, activist, or social justice, curricula skip over the holistic process of self-discovery and development that is a prerequisite for activism.

In other words, activism must come from the students, not the teachers.

The aim of direct action by student groups is only partly to enact change; equally important is the process of shared inquiry that allows students to lead themselves into direct action. Action begins with asking students questions. What are their concerns? What is it about their world that they want to change? What makes them *angry*? What are the pressing questions? What questions and problems make them feel alive? If a classroom can be a space in which these questions are freely asked and answered, a space in which the students' stories are truly heard, then it can also be an effective space to organize.

OIKOS

The liberatory approach to ecology addresses the social inequities connected to the climate crisis. Rather than viewing social justice as something separate from climate change, those crises can be understood as part of the same crisis—the crisis of the cosmology of loneliness. Understandably, students from marginalized communities might feel as though the climate crisis is secondary to their daily concerns of safety and survival. Rather than making arguments against this mentality, it is most important for educators to listen to these perspectives. That said, there are also ways to link a young person's daily struggles to the broader struggles of the planet, just like the struggles of one marginalized group can be connected to another's.

Eco-Justice

In this activity, we have the students line up in a straight line. For each "yes" to the following questions, students take a step forward. See how many students have at least four "yeses."

1. Do you or someone in your family live near a place where there are trucks idling?
2. Do you or someone in your family have asthma?
3. Do you or someone in your family live near a landfill or dump?
4. Do you live near any factories?
5. Do you know anyone who has suffered from lead poisoning?
6. Do you or does anyone in your family have cancer?
7. Do you live in an area where there are no stores with affordable fruits and vegetables?

Have students take a pin and indicate their neighborhood. Map the neighborhoods of those who have four or more yeses and compare to those who have three or less. Would it be as easy to find people to answer "yes" to these questions in a wealthy, white neighborhood? Why?

Plants/Brand Names

This is an activity that I've led with groups of people pretty much from middle school to graduate school. The basic purpose is to better understand where our consciousness is by seeing how much we know about plants versus products.

1. Define what a brand is.
2. Describe what attracts you to certain brands.
3. Identify the impact that brands have on you and others.

Split students into groups. Ask each group to make a list of as many brand names as they can come up with in five minutes. Then do the same with species of plants.

Usually, the list of brands is much longer. Why? What does this say about what we focus on in our lives? What has more value, a plant or a brand name? Discuss the actions of certain popular brands. How does this change your perception of that brand?

Notice how often you are alerted to a brand name in your daily life? What feelings come up as you associate with these brands? Next, try to notice the role of different plant species in your life.

Economics/Ecology

Perhaps no subject could demonstrate the values of our society more than economics. We have made economics primary when it, in fact, describes a subset of ecology. Both come from the Greek word *oikos*, meaning home. Ecology refers to the web of relationships that support life—including us. Our primary home is the ecosystem of which we are a part. Economics originally referred to the way we manage the resources of our home. It now refers to the way the human manages the resources of the planet. Money, an abstraction of these resources, is the primary way to ascribe value to these resources in economics. How does this fail to account for the true value of life? What are your values? What are society's values? How are they different?

Gross Domestic Product

Students explore the values of our culture by studying the GDP (gross domestic product). Some may have heard of it and may know what it stands for, but few will understand what it means for our communities. For most politicians, a growing economy and GDP is the highest value. But the GDP grows for any economic activity. Together, make a list of some things that may not be so positive but grow the GDP:

- Someone gets cancer
- An oil spill
- Someone gets arrested
- A prison is built
- We declare war

Explore one or two of these that have directly affected the students' community. What does this say about our values as a society? What is the difference between equating life or existence with value and the dollar? What are the students' values?

An ecological classroom also must be structured in such a way that, as with an ecosystem, relationships are primary. Justice-making begins seeking fairness and justice in the child's daily life. It begins with all voices being heard. It begins with relationships and community being primary.

CREATIVITY

In Hands above, we addressed what youth activism should not be—initiated and organized by adults. What, then, *is* activism? In part, activism is *play*. Activism is *art*. When a group of young people seek to change their community, world, or classroom, the power of their action resides in the creativity of their protests, the images and stories and songs they might use to create change.

Creativity and art can be a way to foster joy in the process. There is so much despair, so much suffering in the world. While it is important to look honestly at all this, it is equally important to avoid succumbing to despair. We can find beauty in the struggle.

Art is also a way for us to imagine the impossible. Part of the challenge of justice work is that it is often so hard to envision a different kind of world. If we look at our economic system, the values of capitalism are so deeply entrenched in the symbols and stories of the culture, it often seems inevitable, a force of nature. Another way seems impossible.

But the creativity of youth can be a way to envision this alternative world. It is important for teachers to see the classroom as a space for imagining the impossible rather than pushing realism and offering limits. The world beyond the classroom will provide plenty of limitations. The classroom is the place to dream up a new world.

The following is another form of the "I Am" poem that pays special attention to justice and transformation.

Reimagining the "I Am" Poem

The story the world has about me is . . . My story is . . .

> I am (an example of the way I express my wisdom in action)
> I am not (an example of an inaccurate stereotype)
> I am (an example of a species of tree)
> I am (something that you ate)
> I am not (a brand)
> I am (a person or group who has faced oppression or discrimination)
> I am (one word to describe your uniqueness or gift)
> I am (describe your family)
> I am (describe your community)
> I am (describe your world)
> I used to be . . . Now I am . . .

INTEGRATION

Our world is at once given and created. While it is important to have the humility to know we cannot change or control everything, it is equally important to instill in our youth the belief that they can make change. How we educate our children, the kinds of spaces and processes our youth receive growing up, determines the world they will co-create. Liberation begins in the classroom.

Each subject must be a vehicle for liberation, justice, and joy:

> **Cosmos**: Science can and should be a context for advocacy, including eco-justice and the fight against environmental racism as well as the work to seek out more sustainable practices and technologies.
>
> **Arts**: The arts can be a vehicle for social engagement. The activist uses creativity to imagine new possibilities for the future, to critique power and create a vision that people will hear and want to follow, and to bring joy into the process.
>
> **Spirit**: An element of spiritual practice is ethics and justice-making. The tradition of sacred activism, from Martin Luther King Jr. to Gandhi to Thích Nhất Hanh, teaches us that our spirituality isn't merely about life after death or detachment, but also about making a more just world, here and now.
>
> **Hands**: There is an inherent egalitarianism in the shared pursuit of meaningful work and practical life in our classrooms. This offers a new way of being in community.

When these things come together, we are left with a world-vision guided by justice and equality. This is a liberatory process, and one that is never quite finished. But if we enter into it with our whole selves and as a whole community, the process, even if it is painful, can be a joyful one.

Part III

Reimagining the World

One of the great oddities of most educational reform movements is the failure to ask what seems to be the most basic of educational questions: *Why are we educating our children?* The U.S. Department of Education's mission statement is to "promote student achievement and preparation for global competitiveness." This is not only vague; it frames the entire educational process and, I would argue, the broader purpose of our lives in terms of competition. What if the purpose of our lives were joy, or compassion? What if it were something shared rather than a competition? I'd argue that we ought to at least ask the question before we organize any chairs in our classrooms or publish any textbooks. And I'd further argue that the true test of our educational system is not "global competitiveness," but planetary flourishing—a better classroom ought to bring forth a better world.

Chapter 9

Unstandardized Testing

From Classroom to World

Among the more problematic trends in education in recent decades is the rise of high-stakes testing. It's not that testing, even standardized testing, doesn't have a purpose. A test can show us some things about what's working or not working in our schools or for an individual student. But when a test is used as the primary measure of success and failure, it causes several problems.

High-stakes testing, or tests that determine a child's or school's prospects, are inherently unjust. A test is always a limited measure and a score can indicate many things other than the capabilities of the student.

Oddly, standardized tests are used to measure classrooms or schools but are an inherently individualistic endeavor.

Tests are popular precisely because of their limitations. They are designed to seek out that which is testable and, consequently, tend to overvalue those things. The most important things in life—intuition, compassion, wisdom—are quite difficult to test, and are, therefore, ignored by such tests.

And because tests are so overvalued, they tend to skew curricula in this direction. Entire school systems have altered their teaching to fit into the narrow scope of such tests. So, the impact isn't merely on the student or school that does poorly on such a test; pedagogy and curriculum have been altered to accommodate them.

***

A truer test—albeit a harder one to measure—is how the classroom microcosm becomes the world macrocosm. In other words, how does the metaphor we create in the learning space bring forth a better world?

I have described the metaphors of today's conventional classroom as the factory, the prison, and the free market. Let's test those and see how they fare.

The factory model is based on a mechanistic world-vision. Because the classroom itself is seen as something like a machine, the student and the world are envisioned as something like a machine as well. The inherent, organic creativity of child and cosmos are minimized. In viewing the world this way, we have come to see the world as mere machine, something that is valuable only insofar as it is useful. Its sacredness is lost. And, therefore, we have destroyed much of it.

The prison model is based on a dualistic world-vision. The idea of the classroom is not to find joy, connection, or community, but to get out. The classroom focuses on competition that sorts students. Certain select students will have the opportunity to move on, but many will be relegated to systems of punishment. This model yields a world of the chosen and the damned or, to use less theological language, the rich and the poor. It is a system of hierarchy and power.

The free-market model is based on an individualistic world-vision. The classroom, in this model, is primarily a context for competition. It is a radically noncommunal vision of the world, one in which our entire purpose is reduced to economic success and efficiency. This metaphor combines the dualism of the factory model with the hierarchy of the prison model.

Whatever the test scores indicate, I would argue that these metaphorical models have succeeded. For they pass the test of turning classroom metaphor into world-vision. Whatever we think we've been teaching our children, this is what we've really been teaching. And the result is a world that is a factory, a prison, a mall. It is a human who is an isolated individual consumer, a machine, an algorithm, flawed.

***

I wouldn't recommend any test for the subject matter presented in this book. There is no individual test that would be appropriate. For the pedagogy is inherently community oriented. Moreover, an individual's short-term ability to reproduce information or a skill is largely irrelevant. The test is how these subjects bring forth a world, just as the metaphors above brought forth a world based on their values.

While it's never easy to quantify such things or to know precisely how they will play out, I will offer the following 10 questions as a "test" to determine if our classrooms have effectively transitioned into transforming the world.

1. ARE WE AWARE OF THE STORY?

The process of reimagining the classroom begins with an awareness of the deep story that lies beneath our patterns of thought, our politics, our economics. The capitalist system, for example, rests on certain basic assumptions about the world. For it to function, we must believe in the primacy of the individual. Each of us, according to this worldview, is acting primarily as an individual and making choices based on our self-interest. Moreover, it requires us to adhere to a belief that certain things lie outside of the realm of the economy and are, therefore, not relevant.

I'd like to leave aside the merits of such a system for now. As educators, we often move too quickly to push our values onto children. What our children need—and, ultimately, what we need from them—is to gain the capacity to be aware of the underlying story in order to reach their own conclusions. So, when a young person moves through our educational system, they ought to be able to recognize the narrative that lies at the root of a system or policy. This is a requirement for any functioning democracy, but it is also particularly important at this crucial, transitional moment in human history. The old systems and stories are collapsing all around us, along with ecosystems. When we do not understand what's happening, don't realize that there is a story behind our deeply held beliefs, we risk descending into despair, or fascism. Cultivating this awareness is the first function of education.

2. DO WE EXPERIENCE INTIMACY WITH THE EARTH?

Among the fundamental questions for our species at this moment in history is how we can live sustainably on the planet. There are many reasons for the planetary crisis, of course. But on a most fundamental level, they all begin with how we relate to the Earth. Do we see Earth as living and ourselves a part of her? Or do we see the planet as a mere resource to be used and exploited?

Educators often do a great job of helping young people think through practical solutions to the planetary crisis, just as politicians or scientists are good at coming up with practical or policy solutions. But we keep consuming, keep destroying the biosphere. While this has seldom been a part of any school curriculum, part of the work throughout this book has been to help a child know who their kin is. A sense of relationship, of intimacy and kinship with the Earth is the foundation of transformation of consciousness that we need to begin to recognize our place in the world, our connection to the planet from which we cannot separate ourselves.

3. ARE WE PHYSICALLY AND MENTALLY HEALTHY?

Even before the COVID-19 pandemic, we were experiencing pandemics of mental and physical health crises. In wealthy countries like the United States, our children are suffering from an obesity epidemic that brings with it various health problems such as high blood pressure and diabetes. At the same time, even before remote learning, our young people were increasingly depressed, often suicidal, a pattern that seemed to coincide with the rise of smart phones and the proliferation of social media.

What, really, is the point of educating a child if they are to become sick and depressed? No system of education should be considered successful if its students are not physically and emotionally healthy.

The reimagined classroom not only pays attention to the inner life of the child; it weaves the child's inner life into everything and instills in them the recognition of the collective interiority of others. Mental health and wellness—the inner climate—are inextricably linked to the health of the body and of the planet.

4. IS OUR WORK MEANINGFUL AND IMPACTFUL?

So much of the focus of schools is on job preparation and competing in the global economy. Of course, we all want jobs for our children when they finish school. But far too much attention is given to specific jobs, the existence of which, in a rapidly changing world, we really cannot know by the time our children become adults.

It is far better to focus on work rather than jobs. Work is less about feeding the economy than about feeding the soul. But it isn't merely an individual thing. Our work is how we contribute to our community and our world. It is how we *make* our world and how we show, with our hands, what we love and what we value. Work doesn't have to be a job—parenting is work, for example—but it should be respected and honored. And, regardless of salary, it reflects how successful our work in the classroom has been.

5. IS EVERYONE AN ARTIST WHOSE STORY IS HEARD?

Just as we all have work in this world that needs to be done, we all have a story to tell. We are all artists. Our art can take the form of recognized arts like theater or music, but some express their creativity when they cook dinner for their family or build a new bookshelf.

Expressing oneself creatively is healing and restorative. It gives us a physical and emotional outlet. But there is more to it than that. A functioning democracy requires that the voice of the poet is heard. For the artist is one who challenges our assumptions and narratives, who embraces paradox and sees the chaos, complexity, and nuance of our world. The poet is our last defense against fascism; the totalitarian state always comes for the artists first.

If our classroom has done its job, each will see a place for themselves to express themselves in this world. And each will see the need to celebrate the value of art in a democracy.

6. IS EACH PERSON VALUED EQUALLY?

We sat in circles in our classroom because this is how each person could be best seen and heard. While we recognized that each person was different and brought different gifts, we also knew that no one was inherently more valuable—no one *mattered* more—than anyone else.

This isn't a mere teaching tool for a more effective classroom. This is a model for a more just and egalitarian civilization. The more inegalitarian a society is, the less democratic it is. When a person has more value, and therefore more power, because of race or caste or class, we begin to slip from democracy to plutocracy.

Democracy in the United States has always been something toward which we strive rather than a concrete fact. Did we have a true democracy during slavery or Jim Crow? When women couldn't vote? Do we have a democracy now when the government can be bought by the rich?

We ought not assume that because the word democracy is used by the government that we have one. Democracy comes from the circles in our classrooms, and it is lost when we create hierarchical classrooms.

7. ARE WE PLAYING AND LEARNING JOYFULLY?

The classroom should be a space in which curiosity, awe, and wonder are cultivated. And while it is also a place in which to confront difficult and even painful realities and questions, it must not be a place for despair. The classroom should be a place where a person learns how to navigate life's hardships while being lifted up by the community. Above all else, it is where a child must learn that learning and play are one in the same, and that these things require joy.

Too often, we think of the transition into adulthood as a transition away from play. Sure, its forms may change. But we are always students, always learning. And the test of a successful education is our capacity to find joy even as we look honestly at the world's suffering.

8. ARE OUR INSTITUTIONS AND SYSTEMS LIBERATORY?

While we cannot expect absolute equality and justice overnight, these values should guide our institutions. A liberatory classroom is one that strives toward liberation and justice and organizes itself around equality. Its analytical lens is social justice, seeking always to critique power.

Institutions tend to be conservative, tend to reinforce the values, narratives, and power relationships in a society. But this isn't always the case. Just as a classroom can be liberatory, so, too, can a school. So, too, can a government. This isn't about any particular policy. Rather, it means that, collectively, we see the role of our institutions as to remedy inequality and to balance out imbalances of power.

9. ARE OUR STORIES ABOUT OURSELVES ASSET-BASED RATHER THAN DEFICIT-BASED?

Just as our classrooms serve as a model for future institutions, they also serve to tell us something about ourselves. At some point, we each must come to understand who we are and how we got here. Children, particularly marginalized children, are often told that their situation in life is strictly due to their mistakes, to what they lack.

To begin with, this is simply inaccurate. No one comes to their position in life solely due to their own choices or merits. We are deeply interconnected, our stories interwoven.

What's more, to tell a person, repeatedly, that they are fundamentally flawed is profoundly psychologically damaging. We, of course, need to recognize our mistakes and faults. But the core story we each have about ourselves must focus on the gifts we bring if we are ever to heal and reach our potential.

We also miss the gifts that our children bring us if we fail to see them through the asset-based lens. There are ideas that none of us have yet considered, thoughts that have never been shared. If we do not realize that each child brings a universe of wisdom with them, we might miss something that can change the world.

So perhaps the test here is simply to ask a child who they are. We are not our wounds, not our failures—at least not entirely. In our classrooms, each child had something to teach. In our world, each person has a gift to offer.

10. ARE OUR STORIES ABOUT THE WORLD RELATIONAL RATHER THAN THE COSMOLOGY OF LONELINESS?

We began with a story about the world that guided how we thought of the concept of a classroom and how we structure everything in it, from the chairs to the textbooks. This story told us that we were fundamentally alone, essentially lonely. This was the story at the root of both our collective systems—economic and political systems that led us into crises of climate and social justice—and individual psyche—a mentality that has led us to a global mental health crisis.

A classroom serves as a model for the world. Its values become the worldview that determines the kind of world we have. If a child enters a classroom alone, in competition with other children, we have taught them, more than anything in the curriculum, that the world is a lonely place, a context to compete for power and resources.

The alternative is that what is primary in a classroom is not the individuals, not the chairs or desks, not even the curriculum. It is *relationship*. If we can think this way about the classroom, the test of our success will be if we can foster a worldview in which relationship, not possessions or power, is primary.

Epilogue: Learning How to Love and Be Loved

I will end with a call to do the absurd, the impossible. A call to teach that which cannot be taught, to learn that which must be absorbed and felt rather than learned. For in the end, we have arrived at an education that looks nothing like that which we call a school, a classroom that cannot be contained in any room.

Let us ask the questions like this: What makes a good life? What makes a good world? Where can we find beauty and joy? How can a childhood cultivate this discovery?

Let me begin with a memory. It is worth noting that this is not the pathway most schools of education would follow. And I do not mean to reject their ways of knowing, the epistemology that seeks evidence-based practices. Indeed, I am all for evidence. But, as I have argued from the beginning, even the most rigorous evidence requires a story; and even the most compelling story has meaning only when it encounters an open mind and heart, when it comes alive in relationship.

My memory is of my first day of school. This was many years ago, and my mother walked with me. The school, "Number 46" in Rochester, New York, was only a few blocks from my home. I was excited. So excited, in fact, that I ran all the way, ahead of my mother, and barely even said goodbye, shattering her ideas about her firstborn's first day of school.

My mother, for her part, took her disappointment in stride, and put it in the bag with which she carried all her disappointments. And it must have been heavy. She raised two difficult boys without much help or thanks. And she mostly did a great job, I should say. She was my first teacher, and I learned much about words and love from her, things that still matter. One thing I learned from her, for example, was that *if you love someone, you take care of them*. And this was a lesson I take with me throughout my life. I care for the people I love.

But I left off a part of it, the part that I think allowed her to push down—until much later—her disappointment about that first day of kindergarten. She taught me that if you love someone you take care of them—*even if you don't take care of yourself.* I took this lesson with me, too.

And when I began to reflect on this, much later, I realized this was something fundamental that had been left out of my education. I have multiple degrees, some of them from prestigious universities. Generally, I am well respected. But recently, I have encountered challenges for which nothing in my education has prepared me. What good does it do to become educated if we lack the love of our world to apply that education in a way that makes it better?

Still more vexing, what good does it do if we lack the capacity to receive love? The ability to experience joy and to have a healthy and meaningful inner life requires that we learn how to be loved as well as love. We must know both how to give and receive love to put our education into action. This is what facilitates, in the end, the transition from classroom to cosmos, from school to world, from childhood to adulthood.

I keep seeing on social media how we need to teach budgeting or taxes instead of things like algebra. Practical things that we'll use in life. I get it. I never cared much for algebra in school either and haven't used it at all. But we need to be careful about focusing only on the practical: most of us never made money off poetry, but a poem can help us revel in our beauty or sit with our brokenness. More than taxes, I wish I'd learned how to navigate parenthood and marriage and friendship, how to be broken and heal, how to love and be loved. In the end, all the other stuff—taxes and algebra—can be outsourced. But eventually, we've all got to figure out our selves—how to love and heal in a cruel and broken world.

This is perhaps the least quantifiable, least easily explained aspect of raising and educating our children. There is no specific curriculum for it, no simple and straightforward practice. It can be modeled, of course. But even that isn't enough. It is the thing that comes forth in relationship.

Our classrooms are, when all is said and done, a space where stories are told. And these stories are the stuff with which worlds are made. It isn't my job, or anyone else's, to dictate what this story is; by definition, it must emerge in relationship, in process, from our children. But if I were to offer suggestions about what this new cosmo-vision might look like, I might suggest the following.

> It is a story that takes a rigorous look at the creativity of our natural world and connects these observations through a meaningful and coherent narrative.
>
> It is a story of a world created, co-created, and recreated through its intrinsic creativity and honors the work of the poet and artist—the human creators—in perceiving nuance and paradox.
>
> It is a story that recognizes the primacy of relationship and the importance of depth and interiority—mental health is essential.

> It is a story that is told not merely with words and ideas, but also with bodies and hands.
>
> It is a story that is holistic and sees the big picture, but also honors difference and diversity in the endless pursuit of liberation.

But none of these are set in stone, for it is a story that is brought forth in loving relationship. They are decided not in advance, but as the process unfolds.

If we hope to see a world guided by these or similar values, it must begin with classrooms that reflect them. It is through the microcosm of the classroom that the child can first begin to imagine such a world. And to transition from the dreams of the classroom into the world, we must teach our children—show our children—how to give and receive love. This is how these practices become real, how reimagining the classroom allows us to reimagine the world.

References

Ayers, W. and Dohrn, B. (2000). Resisting zero tolerance. *Rethinking Schools* 14 (3).

Barrows, A. and Macy, J. (eds.) (2005). *Rilke's Book of Hours: Love Poems to God*. New York: Riverhead Books.

Berry, T. (1999). *The great work: Our way into the future*. New York: Harmony/Bell Tower.

Boydston, J. (ed.) (2008). *The Middle Works of John Dewey, Volume 9, 1899-1924, Democracy and Education*. Carbondale, IL: Southern Illinois University Press.

Cohen, M.J. (2003). *The Web of Life Imperative: Regenerative Ecopsychology Technology That Help People Think in Balance with Natural Systems*. British Columbia: Trafford.

de Chardin, P.T. (1965). *The Appearance of Man*. New York: Harper & Row.

Edwards, C. (1989). *Van Gogh and God: A Creative Spiritual Quest*. Chicago: Loyola University Press.

Elk, B. and Neihardt, J.G. (2014). *Black Elk Speaks*. Lincoln, NE: Bison Books.

Emersoncentral.com. Circles. https://emersoncentral.com/texts/essays-first-series/circles/ (accessed January 2022).

Evans, K. (2014). Restorative justice—possibilities, but also concerns. Zehr Institute for Restorative Justice Blog (June 26). http://emu.edu/now/restorative-justice/2014/

06/26/restorative-justice-in-education-possibilities-but-also-concerns (accessed January 2022).

Fox, M. (2006). *The A.W.E. Project: Reinventing Education, Reinventing the Human*. Kelowna, British Columbia: CopperHouse.

Fox, M. (2004). *Creativity: Where the Divine and Human Meet*. New York: Penguin.

Fox, M. (1983). *Original Blessing*. New York: Bear & Co.

Garner, H. (2006). *Multiple Intelligences: New Horizons in Theory and Practice*. New York: Basic Books.

Gramsci, A. (1971). *Selections from the Prison Notebooks*. Ann Arbor, MI: University of Michigan.

Maté, G. (2011). *In the Realm of Hungry Ghosts: Close Encounters with Addiction*. Berkeley, CA: North Atlantic Books.

McSweeney, K. (2020). The left brain right brain myth: is it true? https://now.northropgrumman.com/the-left-brain-right-brain-myth-is-it-true/ (accessed January 2022).

Montessori, M. (2012). *The 1946 London Lectures: Volume 17*. Laren, Netherlands: Montessori-Pierson Publishing Company.

Montessori, M (1912). *The Montessori Method*. New York: Frederick A. Stokes.

Montessori, M. (1948). *Reconstruction in Education*. Adyar, India: The Theosophical Publishing House.

Naess, A. (2010). *The Ecology of Wisdom: Writings*. Berkeley. Counterpoint.

Nhêt Hanh, T. (1999). *The Miracle of Mindfulness: An Introduction to the Practice of Meditation*. Boston: Beacon.

Richards, M.C. (2011). *Centering: In Pottery, Poetry, and the Person*. Middletown, CT: Wesleyan University Press.

Richards, T. (2018). *A Letter to My Daughters: Remembering the Lost Dimension & the Texture of Life*. Pawkatuck, CT: Littlebound.

Shiva, V. (2016). *Staying Alive: Women, Ecology and Development.* Berkeley: North Atlantic Books.

Smith, J.A., Newman, K.M., Suttie, J., and Jazaieri, H. (2017). The state of mindfulness science. *Greater Good Magazine* (5 December). https://greatergood.berkeley.edu/article/item/the_state_of_mindfulness_science (accessed January 2022).

U.S. Department of Education. About ED: Mission. https://www2.ed.gov/about/overview/mission/mission.html.

Yazzie, R. (1994). Life Comes from It: Navajo Justice Concepts, 24 N.M. L. Rev. 175 (Spring).

Acknowledgments

At the core of the educational philosophy put forth in this book is the notion that we do nothing in isolation: not teaching, not learning, and not writing a book. This work, therefore, would not be possible without many others, including the following:

My students, who have taught me far more than I have taught them. Above all else, the ideas and practices presented here have emerged from my relationship with them.

The many friends and colleagues who have offered their love, support, and ideas throughout the pandemic and throughout the creation of this book: Theresa McKennie, Ken Wilson, Aisha Baaith Jeffries, Autumn Hernandez, Sara Silvio, Patrick Flynn, Missy Lahren, Matt Switzer, Sam King, Karie Crisp Vazquez, Bryan Pannill, Bill Jordan, Todd Hoskins, and Mollie Dowling.

My mentor, Sue Duncan, who first made me into a teacher.

My teacher, Matthew Fox, who has been a consistent friend and co-conspirator since our days in Oakland with YELLAWE.

The Wisdom Projects staff and board, whose support and friendship over the years has provided the fertile soil for the growth of everything in this book.

My agent, Tim Brandhorst, who has not only helped bring the book to publication but has also been a valued adviser from the very inception of this project.

The Jossey-Bass editorial staff.

Cleis Abeni (tree turtle), co-director of Wisdom Projects, Inc., who has been not only a colleague, but also a friend, providing me with invaluable wisdom and consistent support.

Arianne Richards, my wife, best friend, co-teacher and -parent, who has believed in me and my work from the very beginning, before Wisdom Projects and before I'd ever published anything.

About the Author

Theodore Richards is a writer, philosopher, and educator. He is the founder of The Chicago Wisdom Project and the author of eight books and has received numerous literary awards, including three Independent Publisher Awards and two Nautilus Book Awards. He lives on the south side of Chicago with his wife and three daughters. You can find out more about him and his work at www.theodorerichards.com.

Index

C

D

E

F

I

N

O

S

T

Y

Z